Poems and Ballads

Volume 1 of 2

by
Algernon Charles Swinburne

&
*With a new introduction for this edition
By the editor*

AmunCiné
Wells - Pierce
Boston & Cambridge
2016

TO

MY FRIEND
EDWARD BURNE JONES
THESE POEMS

ARE AFFECTIONATELY AND ADMIRINGLY

DEDICATED.

New Introduction, Design-Graphics
Copyright © 2012 C. A. Strang

Poems, themselves, 1st printed; London; 1904

Introduction

The Swinburne World

Algernon Charles Swinburne (London, 5 April 1837 – London, 10 April 1909)

English poet, playwright, novelist, and critic. He invented the roundel form, wrote several novels, and contributed to the famous 11th of the Encyclopaedia Britannica. He was nominated for the Nobel Prize in Literature in every year from 1903 to 1907 and again in 1909.

Swinburne was born at 7 Chester Street, Grosvenor Place, London, on 5 April 1837. He was the eldest of six children born to Captain (later Admiral) Charles Henry Swinburne and Lady Jane Henrietta, daughter of the 3rd Earl of Ashburnham . He grew up at East Dene in Bonchurch on the Isle of Wight and attended Eton College 1849–53, where he first started writing poetry, and then Balliol College, Oxford 1856–60 with a brief hiatus when he was temporarily expelled from the university in 1859 for having publicly supported the attempted assassination of Napoleon III by Felice Orsini returning in May 1860, though he never received a degree.

He spent summer holidays at Capheaton Hall in Northumberland, the house of his grandfather, Sir John Swinburne, 6th Baronet (1762–1860) who had a famous library and was President of the Literary and Philosophical Society in Newcastle upon Tyne. Swinburne considered Northumberland to be his native county.. He enjoyed riding his pony across the moors (he was a daring horseman) 'through honeyed leagues of the northland border'. He never called it the Scottish border.

At Oxford Swinburne met several Pre-Raphaelites, including Dante Gabriel Rossetti. He also met William Morris. After leaving college he lived in London and started an active writing career, where Rossetti was delighted with his 'little Northumbrian friend', a reference to Swinburne's diminutive height—he was just over five feet tall.

In the years 1857–60, Swinburne became one of Lady Pauline Trevelyan's intellectual circle at Walington Hall and after his grandfather's death in 1860, would stay with William Bell Scott in Newcastle. In December 1862, Swinburne accompanied Scott and his guests, probably including Dante Gabriel Rossetti on a trip to Tynemouth. Scott writes in his memoirs that as they walked by the sea, Swinburne declaimed the as yet unpublished "Hymn to Proserpine" and Laus Veneris".

Decadence Defined: dec-a-dence

1. A process, condition, or period of deterioration or decline, as in morals or art; decay.

2. often Decadence A literary movement especially of late 19th-century France and England characterized by refined aestheticism, artifice, and the quest for new sensations.

[French décadence, from Old French decadence, from Medieval Latin décadentia, a decaying, declining, from Vulgar Latin *décadere, to decay; see decay.]

Oscar Wilde talked of Decadence in the following manner:

* "Classicism is the subordination of the parts to the whole; Decadence is the subordination of the whole to the parts."

Swinburne & The Decadent Movement

"Decadence" as a tag for public artists in any or all of the arts began in the late 18th century, with such early writers as: Jean-Jacques Rousseau (June 28, 1712 – July 2, 1778) and Donatien, Marquis de Sade (June 2, 1740 – December 12, 1814).

But its real hard-core full beginning was the incredible influence of John Polidori (7 September 1795 – 24 August 1821), Mary Wollstonecraft Shelley (30 August 1797 – 1 February 1851), and most importantly – Edgar Allen Poe (January 19, 1809 – October 7, 1849).

"The Second Wave" of Decadents was created by Theophile Gautier (August 30, 1811 – October 23, 1872), Charles Baudelaire (April 9, 1821-August31, 1867), Paul Verlaine (March 30, 1844 – January 8, 1896), and Arthur Rimbaud (October 20, 1854 – November 10, 1891). Gautier and Baudelaire were the first two people to enthusiastically embrace the public name tag as "I am a Decadent!".

The Third Wave was created by Algernon Charles Swinburne, Oscar Wilde, Aubrey Beardsley, Frank Harris, and perhaps John Addington Symonds. In the United States, we could include Harrie & Caresse Crosby – publishers and poets.

The major intellectual tool used by all Decadents was, remains, and is Symbolism.

Symbolism is the oldest and most fundamental method of human expression. Its use of visualization, feelings, and concepts is entirely fluid. Symbolism rarely deals with "equation" and never has "equation" as an integral part of its own process.

Symbolism is an open gateway to creating an instantaneous new way of direct seeing and looking into what we call "reality" but more properly should be called "personal experience". But the paradox is that "this experience" can be directly experienced by others, either as the same experience, or a slightly different form of experience.

The Decay from Decadence is the Birth of the New Highly Needed for the Unborn New to Come

Swinburne's Poetry

Algernon Charles Swinburne almost entirely defies analysis, but sme things can truthfully be said. He manipulates word, vowel, and consonant sound – consider them as 3 separate levels – rather than one single level of sound. He is a post-classist-Hellenic, thus using whole Hellenic structures of thought and emotional response, but also including what I believe is his fascination with the Oracles at Delphi and Cumae, where reason was "bent" to include what could easily be seen as ritual magick and chaos magick. His stances on sexuality and gender are about 150 years before the time when his ideas would come into common agreement with those people who have reject the classical organized Christian religions. Along with Charles Baudelaire, Walt Whitman, and Stephan Crane, he is one of the most radical and mystical poets of the 19th century.

And still in the new 21st century, he still appears as radical, but now there is a great acceptance of his sexual, gender, and spiritual view. Perhaps one might say that Swinburne was a Linguistics Scholar who discovered A world of Freely Rampant Sexuality who lived as a Minor Magistrate in a Small Ancient Greek Town and Who Constantly Wrote Songs the like of which had never before been hear.

And yet it is the music of his words that…….

Caiyros Arlen LeStrang
June 21, 2012

Algernon Charles Swinburne's Works

Verse Drama

- *The Queen Mother* (1860)
- *Rosamond* (1860)
- *Chastelard* (1865)
- *Bothwell* (1874)
- *Mary Stuart* (1881)
- *Marino Faliero* (1885)
- *Locrine* (1887)
- *The Sisters* (1892)
- *Rosamund, Queen of the Lombards* (1899)

Poetry

- *Atalanta in Calydon* (1865) — [although a tragedy, traditionally included with "Poetry"]
- *Poems and Ballads* (1866)
- *Songs Before Sunrise* (1871)
- *Songs of Two Nations* (1875)
- *Erecthus* (1876) — [although a tragedy, traditionally included with "Poetry"]
- *Poems and Ballads, Second Series* (1878)
- *Songs of the Springtides* (1880)
- *Studies in Song* (1880)
- *The Heptalogia, or the Seven against Sense. A Cap with Seven Bells* (1880)
- *Tristam of Lyonesse* (1882)
- *A Century of Roundels* (1883)
- *A Midsummer Holiday and Other Poems* (1884)
- *Poems and Ballads, Third Series* (1889)
- *Astrophel and Other Poems* (1894)
- *The Tale of Balen* (1896)
- *A Channel Passage and Other Poems* (1904)

Criticism

- *William Blake: A Critical Essay* (1868, new edition 1906)
- *Under the Microscope* (1872)
- *George Chapman: A Critical Essay* (1875)
- *Essays and Studies* (1875)
- *A Note on Charlotte Brontë* (1877)
- *A Study of Shakespeare* (1880)
- *A Study of Victor Hugo* (1886)
- *A Study of Ben Johnson* (1889)
- *Studies in Prose and Poetry* (1894)
- *The Age of Shakespeare* (1908)
- *Shakespeare* (1909)

DEDICATORY EPISTLE

TO THEODORE WATTS-DUNTON

To my best and dearest friend [ed. Note: "and Lover"], I dedicate the first collected edition of my poems, and to him I address what I have to say on the occasion.

You will agree with me that it is impossible for any man to undertake the task of commentary, however brief and succinct, on anything he has done or tried to do, without incurring the charge of egoism. But there are two kinds of egoism, the furtive and the frank: and the outspoken and open-hearted candour of Milton and Wordsworth, Corneille and Hugo, is not the least or the lightest of their claims to the regard as well as the respect or the reverence of their readers. Even if I were worthy to claim kinship with the lowest or with the highest of these deathless names, I would not seek to shelter myself under the shadow of its authority. The question would still remain open on all sides. Whether it is worthwhile for any man to offer any remarks or for any other man to read his remarks on his own work, his own ambition, or his own attempts, he cannot of course determine.

If there are great examples of abstinence from such a doubtful enterprise, there are likewise great examples to the contrary. As long as the writer can succeed in evading the kindred charges and the cognate risks of vanity and humility, there can be no reason why he should not undertake it. And when he has nothing to regret and nothing to recant, when he finds nothing that he could wish to cancel, to alter, or to unsay, in any page he has ever laid before his reader, he need not be seriously troubled by the inevitable consciousness that the work of his early youth is not and cannot be unnaturally unlike the work of a very young man. This would be no excuse for it, if it were in any sense bad work: if it be so, no apology would avail; and I certainly have none to offer.

It is now thirty-six years since my first volume of miscellaneous verse, lyrical and dramatic and elegiac and generally heterogeneous, had as quaint a reception and as singular a fortune as I have ever heard or read of. I do not think you will differ from my opinion that what is best in it cannot be divided from what is not so good by any other line of division than that which marks off mature from immature execution—in other words, complete from incomplete conception. For its author the most amusing and satisfying result of the clatter aroused by it was the deep diversion of collating and comparing the variously inaccurate verdicts of the scornful or mournful censors who insisted on regarding all the studies of passion or sensation attempted or achieved in it as either confessions of positive fact or excursions of absolute fancy. There are photographs from life in the book; and there are sketches from imagination. Some which keen-sighted criticism has dismissed with a smile as ideal or imaginary were as real and actual as they well could be: others which have been taken for obvious transcripts from memory were utterly fantastic or dramatic.

If the two kinds cannot be distinguished, it is surely rather a credit than a discredit to an artist whose medium or material has more in common with a musician's than with a sculptor's. Friendly and kindly critics, English and foreign, have detected ignorance of the subject in poems taken straight from the life, and have protested that they could not believe me were I to swear that poems entirely or mainly fanciful were not faithful expressions or transcriptions of the writer's actual experience and personal emotion.

But I need not remind you that all I have to say about this book was said once for all in the year of its publication: I have nothing to add to my notes then taken, and I have nothing to retract from them. To parade or to disclaim experience of passion or of sorrow, of pleasure or of pain, is the habit and the sign of a school which has never found a disciple among the better sort of English poets, and which I know to be no less pitifully contemptible in your opinion than in mine.

In my next work it should be superfluous to say that there is no touch of dramatic impersonation or imaginary emotion. The writer of 'Songs before Sunrise,' from the first line to the last, wrote simply in submissive obedience to Sir Philip Sidney's precept—'Look in thine heart, and write.'

The dedication of these poems, and the fact that the dedication was accepted, must be sufficient evidence of this. They do not pretend and they were never intended to be merely the metrical echoes, or translations into lyric verse, of another man's doctrine. Mazzini was no more a Pope or a Dictator than I was a parasite or a papist. Dictation and inspiration are rather different things.

These poems, and others which followed or preceded them in print, were inspired by such faith as is born of devotion and reverence: not by such faith, if faith it may be called, as is synonymous with servility or compatible with prostration of an abject or wavering spirit and a submissive or dethroned intelligence. You know that I never pretended to see eye to eye with my illustrious friends and masters, Victor Hugo and Giuseppe Mazzini, in regard to the positive and passionate confidence of their sublime and purified theology.

Our betters ought to know better than we: they would be the last to wish that we should pretend to their knowledge, or assume a certitude which is theirs and is not ours. But on one point we surely cannot but be at one with them: that the spirit and the letter of all other than savage and barbarous religions are irreconcilably at variance, and that prayer or homage addressed to an image of our own or of other men's making, be that image avowedly material or conventionally spiritual, is the affirmation of idolatry with all its attendant atrocities, and the negation of all belief, all reverence, and all love, due to the noblest object of human worship that humanity can realise or conceive.

Thus much the exercise of our common reason might naturally suffice to show us: but when its evidence is confirmed and fortified by the irrefragable and invariable evidence of history, there is no room for further dispute or fuller argument on a subject now visibly beyond reach and eternally beyond need of debate or demonstration. I know not whether it may or may not be worthwhile to add that every passing word I have since thought fit to utter on any national or political question has been as wholly consistent with the principles which I then did my best to proclaim and defend as any apostasy from the faith of all republicans in the fundamental and final principle of union, voluntary if possible and compulsory if not, would have been ludicrous in the impudence of its inconsistency with those simple and irreversible principles.

Monarchists and anarchists may be advocates of national dissolution and reactionary division: republicans cannot be. The first and last article of their creed is unity: the most grinding and crushing tyranny of a convention, a directory, or a despot, is less incompatible with republican faith than the fissiparous democracy of disunionists or communalists.

If the fortunes of my lyrical work were amusingly eccentric and accidental, the varieties of opinion which have saluted the appearance of my plays have been, or have seemed to my humility, even more diverting and curious. I have been told by reviewers of note and position that a single one of them is worth all my lyric and otherwise undramatic achievements or attempts: and I have been told on equal or similar authority that, whatever I may be in any other field, as a dramatist I am demonstrably nothing.

My first if not my strongest ambition was to do something worth doing, and not utterly unworthy of a young countryman of Marlowe the teacher and Webster the pupil of Shakespeare, in the line of work which those three poets had left as a possibly unattainable example for ambitious Englishmen. And my first book, written while yet under academic or tutorial authority, bore evidence of that ambition in every line. I should be the last to deny that it also bore evidence of the fact that its writer had no more notion of dramatic or theatrical construction than the authors of 'Tamburlaine the Great,' 'King Henry VI.,' and 'Sir Thomas Wyatt.' Not much more, you may possibly say, was discernible in 'Chastelard': a play also conceived and partly written by a youngster not yet emancipated from servitude to college rule. I fear that in the former volume there had been little if any promise of power to grapple with the realities and subtleties of character and of motive: that whatever may be in it of promise or of merit must be sought in the language and the style of such better passages as may perhaps be found in single and separable speeches of Catherine and of Rosamond.

But in 'Chastelard' there are two figures and a sketch in which I certainly seem to see something of real and evident life. The sketch of Darnley was afterwards filled out and finished in the subsequent tragedy of 'Bothwell.' That ambitious, conscientious, and comprehensive piece of work is of course less properly definable as a tragedy than by the old Shakespearean term of a chronicle history. The radical difference between tragic history and tragedy of either the classic or the romantic order, and consequently between the laws which govern the one and the principles which guide the other, you have yourself made clear and familiar to all capable students. This play of mine was not, I think, inaccurately defined as an epic drama in the French verses of dedication which were acknowledged by the greatest of all French poets in a letter from which I dare only quote one line of Olympian judgment and godlike generosity. 'Occuper ces deux cimes, cela n'est donné qu'à vous.'

Nor will I refrain from the confession that I cannot think it an epic or a play in which any one part is sacrificed to any other, any subordinate figure mishandled or neglected or distorted or effaced for the sake of the predominant and central person.

And, though this has nothing or less than nothing to do with any question of poetic merit or demerit, of dramatic success or unsuccess, I will add that I took as much care and pains as though I had been writing or compiling a history of the period to do loyal justice to all the historic figures which came within the scope of my dramatic or poetic design.

There is not one which I have designedly altered or intentionally modified: it is of course for others to decide whether there is one which is not the living likeness of an actual or imaginable man.

The third part of this trilogy, as far as I know or remember, found favour only with the only man in England who could speak on the subject of historic drama with the authority of an expert and a master. The generally ungracious reception of 'Mary Stuart' gave me neither surprise nor disappointment: the cordial approbation or rather the generous applause of Sir Henry Taylor gave me all and more than all the satisfaction I could ever have looked for in recompense of as much painstaking and conscientious though interesting and enjoyable work as can ever, I should imagine, have been devoted to the completion of any comparable design. Private and personal appreciation I have always thought and often found more valuable and delightful than all possible or imaginable clamour of public praise. This preference will perhaps be supposed to influence my opinion if I avow that I think I have never written anything worthier of such reward than the closing tragedy which may or may not have deserved but which certainly received it.

My first attempt to do something original in English which might in some degree reproduce for English readers the likeness of a Greek tragedy, with possibly something more of its true poetic life and charm than could have been expected from the authors of 'Caractacus' and 'Merope,' was perhaps too exuberant and effusive in its dialogue, as it certainly was too irregular in the occasional license of its choral verse, to accomplish the design or achieve the success which its author should have aimed at. It may or may not be too long as a poem: it is, I fear, too long for a poem of the kind to which it belongs or aims at belonging. Poetical and mathematical truth are so different that I doubt, however unwilling I may naturally be to doubt, whether it can truthfully be said of 'Atalanta in Calydon' that the whole is greater than any part of it.
I hope it may be, and I can honestly say no more. Of 'Erechtheus' I venture to believe with somewhat more confidence that it can. Either poem, by the natural necessity of its kind and structure, has its crowning passage or passages which cannot, however much they may lose by

detachment from their context, lose as much as the crowning scene or scenes of an English or Shakespearean play, as opposed to an Æschylean or Sophoclean tragedy, must lose and ought to lose by a similar separation. The two best things in these two Greek plays, the antiphonal lamentation for the dying Meleager and the choral presentation of stormy battle between the forces of land and sea, lose less by such division from the main body of the poem than would those scenes in 'Bothwell' which deal with the turning-point in the life of Mary Stuart on the central and conclusive day of Carberry Hill.

It might be thought pedantic or pretentious in a modern poet to divide his poems after the old Roman fashion into sections and classes; I must confess that I should like to see this method applied, were it but by way of experiment in a single edition, to the work of the leading poets of our own country and century: to see, for instance, their lyrical and elegiac works ranged and registered apart, each kind in a class of its own, such as is usually reserved, I know not why, for sonnets only.
The apparent formality of such an arrangement as would give us, for instance, the odes of Coleridge and Shelley collected into a distinct reservation or division might possibly be more than compensated to the more capable among students by the gain in ethical or spiritual symmetry and æsthetic or intellectual harmony.

The ode or hymn—I need remind no probable reader that the terms are synonymous in the speech of Pindar—asserts its primacy or pre-eminence over other forms of poetry in the very name which defines or proclaims it as essentially the song; as something above all less pure and absolute kinds of song by the very nature and law of its being.

The Greek form, with its regular arrangement of turn, return, and aftersong, is not to be imitated because it is Greek, but to be adopted because it is best: the very best, as a rule, that could be imagined for lyrical expression of the thing conceived or lyrical aspiration towards the aim imagined.

The rhythmic reason of its rigid but not arbitrary law lies simply and solely in the charm of its regular variations. This can be given in English as clearly and fully, if not so sweetly and subtly, as in Greek; and should, therefore, be expected and required in an English poem of the same nature and proportion.

The Sapphic or Alcaic ode, a simple sequence of identical stanzas, could be imitated or revived in Latin by translators or disciples: the scheme of it is exquisitely adequate and sufficient for comparatively short flights of passion or emotion, ardent or contemplative and personal or patriotic; but what can be done in English could not be attempted in Latin.
It seems strange to me, our language being what it is, that our literature should be no richer than it is in examples of the higher or at least the more capacious and ambitious kind of ode.

Not that the full Pindaric form of threefold or triune structure need be or should be always adopted: but without an accurately corresponsive or antiphonal scheme of music even the master of masters, who is Coleridge, could not produce, even through the superb and enchanting melodies of such a poem as his 'Dejection,' a fit and complete companion, a full and perfect rival, to such a poem as his ode on France.

The title of ode may more properly and fairly be so extended as to cover all lyrical poems in stanzas or couplets than so strained as to include a lawless lyric of such irregular and uneven build as Coleridge only and hardly could make acceptable or admissible among more natural and lawful forms of poetry. Law, not lawlessness, is the natural condition of poetic life; but the law must itself be poetic and not pedantic, natural and not conventional.

It would be a trivial precision or restriction which would refuse the title of ode to the stanzas of Milton or the heptameters of Aristophanes; that glorious form of lyric verse which a critic of our own day, as you may not impossibly remember, has likened with such magnificent felicity of comparison to the gallop of the horses of the sun.

Nor, I presume, should this title be denied to a poem written in the more modest metre—more modest as being shorter by a foot—which was chosen for those twin poems of antiphonal correspondence in subject and in sound, the 'Hymn to Proserpine' and the 'Hymn of Man': the deathsong of spiritual decadence and the birthsong of spiritual renascence.

Perhaps, too, my first stanzas addressed to Victor Hugo may be ranked as no less of an ode than that on the insurrection in Candia: a poem which attracted, whether or not it may have deserved, the notice and commendation of Mazzini: from whom I received, on the occasion of its appearance, a letter which was the beginning of my personal intercourse with the man whom I had always revered above all other men on earth.

But for this happy accident I might not feel disposed to set much store by my first attempt at a regular ode of orthodox or legitimate construction; I doubt whether it quite succeeded in evading the criminal risk and the capital offence of formality; at least until the change of note in the closing epode gave fuller scope and freer play of wing to the musical expression.

But in my later ode on Athens, absolutely faithful as it is in form to the strictest type and the most stringent law of Pindaric hymnology, I venture to believe that there is no more sign of this infirmity than in the less classically regulated poem on the Armada; which, though built on a new scheme, is nevertheless in its way, I think, a legitimate ode, by right of its regularity in general arrangement of corresponsive divisions.

By the test of these two poems I am content that my claims should be decided and my station determined as a lyric poet in the higher sense of the term; a craftsman in the most ambitious line of his art that ever aroused or ever can arouse the emulous aspiration of his kind.

Even had I ever felt the same impulse to attempt and the same ambition to achieve the enterprise of epic or narrative that I had always felt with regard to lyric or dramatic work, I could never have proposed to myself the lowly and unambitious aim of competition with the work of so notable a contemporary workman in the humbler branch of that line as William Morris. No conception could have been further from my mind when I undertook to rehandle the deathless legend of Tristram than that of so modest and preposterous a trial of rivalry.

My aim was simply to present that story, not diluted and debased as it had been in our own time by other hands, but undefaced by improvement and undeformed by transformation, as it was known to the age of Dante wherever the chronicles of romance found hearing, from

Ercildoune to Florence: and not in the epic or romantic form of sustained or continuous narrative, but mainly through a succession of dramatic scenes or pictures with descriptive settings or backgrounds: the scenes being of the simplest construction, duologue or monologue, without so much as the classically permissible intervention of a third or fourth person. It is only in our native northern form of narrative poetry, on the old and unrivaled model of the English ballad, that I can claim to have done any work of the kind worth reference: unless the story of Balen should be considered as something other than a series or sequence of ballads.

A more plausible objection was brought to bear against 'Tristram of Lyonesse' than that of failure in an enterprise which I never thought of undertaking: the objection of an irreconcilable incongruity between the incidents of the old legend and the meditations on man and nature, life and death, chance and destiny, assigned to a typical hero of chivalrous romance. And this objection might be unanswerable if the slightest attempt had been made to treat the legend as in any possible sense historical or capable of either rational or ideal association with history, such as would assimilate the name and fame of Arthur to the name and fame of any actual and indisputable Alfred or Albert of the future.

But the age when these romances actually lived and flourished side by side with the reviving legends of Thebes and Troy, not in the crude and bloodless forms of Celtic and archaic fancy but in the ampler and manlier developments of Teutonic and mediaeval imagination, was the age of Dante and of Chaucer: an age in which men were only too prone to waste their time on the twin sciences of astrology and theology, to expend their energies in the jungle of pseudosophy or the morass of metaphysics.

There is surely nothing more incongruous or anachronic in the soliloquy of Tristram after his separation from Iseult than in the lecture of Theseus after the obsequies of Arcite. Both heroes belong to the same impossible age of an imaginary world: and each has an equal right, should it so please his chronicler, to reason in the pauses of action and philosophize in the intervals of adventure. After all, the active men of the actual age of chivalry were not all of them mere muscular machines for martial or pacific exercise of their physical functions or abilities.

You would agree, if the point were worth discussion, that it might savour somewhat of pretension, if not of affectation, to be over particular in arrangement of poems according to subject rather than form, spirit rather than method, or motive rather than execution: and yet there might be some excuse for the fancy or the pedantry of such a classification as should set apart, for example, poems inspired by the influence of places, whether seen but once or familiar for years or associated with the earliest memories within cognizance or record of the mind, and poems inspired by the emotions of regard or regret for the living or the dead; above all, by the rare and profound passion of reverence and love and faith which labours and rejoices to find utterance in some tributary sacrifice of song. Mere descriptive poetry of the prepense and formal kind is exceptionally if not proverbially liable to incur and to deserve the charge of dullness: it is unnecessary to emphasize or obtrude the personal note, the presence or the emotion of a spectator, but it is necessary to make it felt and keep it perceptible if the poem is to have life in it or even a right to live: felt as in Wordsworth's work it is always, perceptible as it is always in Shelley's.

This note is more plain and positive than usual in the poem which attempts—at once a simple and an ambitious attempt—to render the contrast and the concord of night and day on Loch Torridon: it is, I think, duly sensible though implicitly subdued in four poems of the West Undercliff, born or begotten of sunset in the bay and moonlight on the cliffs, noon or morning in a living and shining garden, afternoon or twilight on one left flowerless and forsaken.

Not to you or any other poet, nor indeed to the very humblest and simplest lover of poetry, will it seem incongruous or strange, suggestive of imperfect sympathy with life or deficient inspiration from nature, that the very words of Sappho should be heard and recognized in the notes of the nightingales, the glory of the presence of dead poets imagined in the presence of the glory of the sky, the lustre of their advent and their passage felt visible as in vision on the live and limpid floor work of the cloudless and sunset-coloured sea.
The half-brained creature to whom books are other than living things may see with the eyes of a bat and draw with the fingers of a mole his dullard's distinction between books and life: those who live the fuller life of a higher animal than he know that books are to poets as much part of that life as pictures are to painters or as music is to musicians, dead matter though they may be to the spiritually still-born children of dirt and dullness who find it possible and natural to live while dead in heart and brain. Marlowe and Shakespeare, Æschylus and Sappho, do not for us live only on the dusty shelves of libraries.

It is hardly probable that especial and familiar love of places should give any special value to verses written under the influence of their charm: no intimacy of years and no association with the past gave any colour of emotion to many other studies of English land and sea which certainly are no less faithful and possibly have no less spiritual or poetic life in them than the four to which I have just referred, whose localities lie all within the boundary of a mile or so.

No contrast could be stronger than that between the majestic and exquisite glory of cliff and crag, lawn and woodland, garden and lea, to which I have done homage though assuredly I have not done justice in these four poems—'In the Bay,' 'On the Cliffs,' 'A Forsaken Garden,' the dedication of 'The Sisters'—and the dreary beauty, inhuman if not unearthly in its desolation, of the innumerable creeks and inlets, lined and paven with sea-flowers, which make of the salt marshes a fit and funereal setting, a fatal and appropriate foreground, for the supreme desolation of the relics of Dunwich; the beautiful and awful solitude of a wilderness on which the sea has forbidden man to build or live, overtopped and bounded by the tragic and ghastly solitude of a headland on which the sea has forbidden the works of human charity and piety to survive: between the dense and sand-encumbered tides which are eating the desecrated wreck and ruin of them all away, and the matchless magic, the ineffable fascination of the sea whose beauties and delights, whose translucent depths of water and divers-coloured banks of submarine foliage and flowerage, but faintly reflected in the stanzas of the little ode 'Off Shore,' complete the charm of the scenes as faintly sketched or shadowed forth in the poems just named, or the sterner and stranger magic of the seaboard to which tribute was paid in 'An Autumn Vision,' 'A Swimmer's Dream,' 'On the South Coast,' 'Neap-tide': or, again, between the sterile stretches and sad limitless outlook of the shore which faces a hitherto undetermined and interminable sea, and the joyful and fateful beauty of the seas off Bamborough and the seas about Sark and Guernsey.

But if there is enough of the human or personal note to bring into touch the various poems which deal with these various impressions, there may perhaps be no less of it discernible in such as try to render the effect of inland or woodland solitude—the splendid oppression of nature at noon which found utterance of old in words of such singular and everlasting significance as panic and nympholepsy.

The retrospect across many years over the many eulogistic and elegiac poems which I have inscribed or devoted to the commemoration or the panegyric of the living or the dead has this in it of pride and pleasure, that I find little to recant and nothing to repent on reconsideration of them all.

If ever a word of tributary thanksgiving for the delight and the benefit of loyal admiration evoked in the spirit of a boy or aroused in the intelligence of a man may seem to exceed the limit of demonstrable accuracy, I have no apology to offer for any such aberration from the safe path of tepid praise or conventional applause. I can truly say with Shelley that I have been fortunate in friendships: I might add if I cared, as he if he had cared might have added, that I have been no less fortunate in my enemies than in my friends; and this, though by comparison a matter of ineffable insignificance, can hardly be to any rational and right-minded man a matter of positive indifference. Rather should it be always a subject for thankfulness and self-congratulation if a man can honestly and reasonably feel assured that his friends and foes alike have been always and at almost all points the very men he would have chosen, had choice and foresight been allowed him, at the very outset of his career in life.

I should never, when a boy, have dared to dream that as a man I might possibly be admitted to the personal acquaintance of the three living gods, I do not say of my idolatry, for idolatry is a term inapplicable where the gods are real and true, but of my whole-souled and single-hearted worship: and yet, when writing of Landor, of Mazzini, and of Hugo, I write of men who have honoured me with the assurance and the evidence of their cordial and affectionate regard. However inadequate and unworthy may be my tribute to their glory when living and their memory when dead, it is that of one whose gratitude and devotion found unforgettable favour in their sight.

And I must be allowed to add that the redeeming quality of entire and absolute sincerity may be claimed on behalf of every line I have written in honour of friends, acquaintances, or strangers. My tribute to Richard Burton was not more genuine in its expression than my tribute to Christina Rossetti. Two noble human creatures more utterly unlike each other it would be unspeakably impossible to conceive; but it was as simply natural for one who honoured them both to do honest homage, before and after they had left us, to the saintly and secluded poetess as to the adventurous and unsaintly hero. Wherever anything is worthy of honour and thanksgiving it is or it always should be as natural if not as delightful to give thanks and do honour to a stranger as to a friend, to a benefactor long since dead as to a benefactor still alive.

To the kindred spirits of Philip Sidney and Aurelio Saffi it was almost as equal a pleasure to offer what tribute I could bring as if Sidney also could have honoured me with his personal friendship. To Tennyson and Browning it was no less fit that I should give honour than that I should do homage to the memory of Bruno, the martyred friend of Sidney. And I can hardly remember any task that I ever took more delight in discharging than I felt in the inadequate and partial payment of a lifelong debt to the marvellous and matchless succession of poets who made the glory of our country incomparable forever by the work they did between the joyful date of the rout of the Armada and the woful date of the outbreak of civil war.

Charles Lamb, as I need not remind you, wrote for antiquity: nor need you be assured that when I write plays it is with a view to their being acted at the Globe, the Red Bull, or the Black Friars. And whatever may be the dramatic or other defects of 'Marino Faliero' or 'Locrine,' they do certainly bear the same relation to previous plays or attempts at plays on the same subjects as 'King Henry V.' to 'The Famous Victories'—if not as 'King Lear,' a poem beyond comparison with all other works of man except possibly 'Prometheus' and 'Othello,' to the primitive and infantile scrawl or drivel of 'King Leir and his three daughters.'

The fifth act of 'Marino Faliero,' hopelessly impossible as it is from the point of view of modern stagecraft, could hardly have been found too untheatrical, too utterly given over to talk without action, by the audiences which endured and applauded the magnificent monotony of Chapman's eloquence—the fervent and inexhaustible declamation which was offered and accepted as a substitute for study of character and interest of action when his two finest plays, if plays they can be called, found favour with an incredibly intelligent and an inconceivably tolerant audience.

The metrical or executive experiment attempted and carried through in 'Locrine' would have been improper to any but a purely and wholly romantic play or poem: I do not think that the life of human character or the lifelikeness of dramatic dialogue has suffered from the bondage of rhyme or has been sacrificed to the exigence of metre. The tragedy of 'The Sisters,' however defective it may be in theatrical interest or progressive action, is the only modern English play I know in which realism in the reproduction of natural dialogue and accuracy in the representation of natural intercourse between men and women of gentle birth and breeding have been found or made compatible with expression in genuine if simple blank verse.

It is not for me to decide whether anything in the figures which play their parts on my imaginary though realistic stage may be worthy of sympathy, attention, or interest: but I think they talk and act as they would have done in life without ever lapsing into platitude or breaking out of nature.

In 'Rosamund, Queen of the Lombards,' I took up a subject long since mishandled by an English dramatist of all but the highest rank, and one which in later days Alfieri had commemorated in a magnificent passage of a wholly unhistoric and somewhat unsatisfactory play. The comparatively slight deviation from historic records in the final catastrophe or consummation of mine is not, I think, to say the least, injurious to the tragic effect or the moral interest of the story.

A writer conscious of any natural command over the musical resources of his language can hardly fail to take such pleasure in the enjoyment of this gift or instinct as the greatest writer and the greatest versifier of our age must have felt at its highest possible degree when composing a musical exercise of such incomparable scope and fullness as 'Les Djinns.'

But if he be a poet after the order of Hugo or Coleridge or Shelley, the result will be something very much more than a musical exercise; though indeed, except to such ears as should always be kept closed against poetry, there is no music in verse which has not in it sufficient fullness and ripeness of meaning, sufficient adequacy of emotion or of thought, to abide the analysis of any other than the purblind scrutiny of prepossession or the squint-eyed inspection of malignity.

There may perhaps be somewhat more depth and variety of feeling or reflection condensed into the narrow frame of the poems which compose 'A Century of Roundels' than would be needed to fulfill the epic vacuity of a Chœrilus or a Coluthus. And the form chosen for my only narrative poem was chosen as a test of the truth of my conviction that such work could be done better on the straitest and the strictest principles of verse than on the looser and more slippery lines of mediaeval or modern improvisation.
The impulsive and irregular verse which had been held sufficient for the stanza selected or accepted by Thornton and by Tennyson seemed capable of improvement and invigoration as a vehicle or a medium for poetic narrative. And I think it has not been found unfit to give something of dignity as well as facility to a narrative which recasts in modern English verse one of the noblest and loveliest old English legends.

There is no episode in the cycle of Arthurian romance more genuinely Homeric in its sublime simplicity and its pathetic sublimity of submission to the masterdom of fate than that which I have rather reproduced than recast in 'The Tale of Balen': and impossible as it is to render the text or express the spirit of the Iliad in English prose or rhyme—above all, in English blank verse—it is possible, in such a metre as was chosen and refashioned for this poem, to give some sense of the rage and rapture of battle for which Homer himself could only find fit and full expression by similitudes drawn like mine from the revels and the terrors and the glories of the sea.

It is nothing to me that what I write should find immediate or general acceptance: it is much to know that on the whole it has won for me the right to address this dedication and inscribe this edition to you.

TABLE of CONTENTS

Introduction	3
Decadence Defined: dec-a-dence	5
Swinburne & The Decadent Movement	6
Swinburne's Poetry	8
Algernon Charles Swinburne's Works	9
DEDICATORY EPISTLE	11
TABLE of CONTENTS	32
A BALLAD OF LIFE	35
A BALLAD OF DEATH	38
LAUS VENERIS	42
LAUS VENERIS	43
EXPLICIT LAUS VENERIS	58
THE TRIUMPH OF TIME	65
LES NOYADES	78
A LEAVE-TAKING	81
ITYLUS	83
ANACTORIA	85
HYMN TO PROSERPINE	94
EPICTETUS	101
HERMAPHRODITUS	106
FRAGOLETTA	108
RONDEL	111
SATIA TE SANGUINE	112
A LITANY	115
A LAMENTATION	120
ANIMA ANCEPS	124
IN THE ORCHARD	126
A MATCH	128
FAUSTINE	130
SONG BEFORE DEATH	137
ROCOCO	138
STAGE LOVE	141
THE LEPER	142
A BALLAD OF BURDENS	148
RONDEL	151

BEFORE THE MIRROR	152
EROTION	155
IN MEMORY OF WALTER SAVAGE LANDOR	157
A SONG IN TIME OF ORDER. 1852	159
A SONG IN TIME OF REVOLUTION. 1860	161
TO VICTOR HUGO	165
BEFORE DAWN	172
DOLORES	175
THE GARDEN OF PROSERPINE	189
HESPERIA	193
LOVE AT SEA	199
APRIL	201
BEFORE PARTING	204
THE SUNDEW	206
FÉLISE	208
AN INTERLUDE	218
HENDECASYLLABICS	220
SAPPHICS	222
AT ELEUSIS	225
AUGUST	232
A CHRISTMAS CAROL	234
THE MASQUE OF QUEEN BERSABE	237
ST. DOROTHY	254
THE TWO DREAMS	268
AHOLIBAH	281
LOVE AND SLEEP	287
MADONNA MIA	288
THE KING'S DAUGHTER	291
AFTER DEATH	293
MAY JANET	296
THE BLOODY SON	298
THE SEA-SWALLOWS	301
THE YEAR OF LOVE	304
DEDICATION 1865	306

Poems & Ballads

A BALLAD OF LIFE

I found in dreams a place of wind and flowers,
  Full of sweet trees and colour of glad grass,
  In midst whereof there was
A lady clothed like summer with sweet hours.
Her beauty, fervent as a fiery moon,
  Made my blood burn and swoon
    Like a flame rained upon.
Sorrow had filled her shaken eyelids' blue,
And her mouth's sad red heavy rose all through
    Seemed sad with glad things gone.

She held a little cithern by the strings,
  Shaped heartwise, strung with subtle-coloured hair
  Of some dead lute-player
That in dead years had done delicious things.
The seven strings were named accordingly;
  The first string charity,
    The second tenderness,
The rest were pleasure, sorrow, sleep, and sin,
And loving-kindness, that is pity's kin
    And is most pitiless.

There were three men with her, each garmented
  With gold and shod with gold upon the feet;
  And with plucked ears of wheat
The first man's hair was wound upon his head:
His face was red, and his mouth curled and sad;
  All his gold garment had
    Pale stains of dust and rust.
A riven hood was pulled across his eyes;
The token of him being upon this wise
    Made for a sign of Lust.

The next was Shame, with hollow heavy face

   Coloured like green wood when flame kindles it.
  He hath such feeble feet
They may not well endure in any place.
His face was full of grey old miseries,
  And all his blood's increase
    Was even increase of pain.
The last was Fear, that is akin to Death;
He is Shame's friend, and always as Shame saith
    Fear answers him again.

My soul said in me; This is marvelous,
  Seeing the air's face is not so delicate
  Nor the sun's grace so great,
If sin and she be kin or amorous.
And seeing where maidens served her on their knees,
  I bade one crave of these
    To know the cause thereof.
Then Fear said: I am Pity that was dead.
And Shame said: I am Sorrow comforted.
    And Lust said: I am Love.

Thereat her hands began a lute-playing
  And her sweet mouth a song in a strange tongue;
  And all the while she sung
There was no sound but long tears following
Long tears upon men's faces, waxen white
  With extreme sad delight.
    But those three following men
Became as men raised up among the dead;
Great glad mouths open and fair cheeks made red
    With child's blood come again.

Then I said: Now assuredly I see
  My lady is perfect, and transfigureth
  All sin and sorrow and death,
Making them fair as her own eyelids be,

Or lips wherein my whole soul's life abides;
  Or as her sweet white sides
    And bosom carved to kiss.
Now therefore, if her pity further me,
Doubtless for her sake all my days shall be
    As righteous as she is.

Forth, ballad, and take roses in both arms,
  Even till the top rose touch thee in the throat
Where the least thorn prick harms;
  And girdled in thy golden singing-coat,
Come thou before my lady and say this;
  Borgia, thy gold hair's colour burns in me,
    Thy mouth makes beat my blood in feverish rhymes;
  Therefore so many as these roses be,
    Kiss me so many times.
Then it may be, seeing how sweet she is,
  That she will stoop herself none otherwise
    Than a blown vine-branch doth,
  And kiss thee with soft laughter on thine eyes,
    Ballad, and on thy mouth.

A BALLAD OF DEATH

Kneel down, fair Love, and fill thyself with tears,
Girdle thyself with sighing for a girth
Upon the sides of mirth,
Cover thy lips and eyelids, let thine ears
Be filled with rumour of people sorrowing;
Make thee soft raiment out of woven sighs
Upon the flesh to cleave,
Set pains therein and many a grievous thing,
And many sorrows after each his wise
For armlet and for gorget and for sleeve.

O Love's lute heard about the lands of death,
Left hanged upon the trees that were therein;
O Love and Time and Sin,
Three singing mouths that mourn now underbreath,
Three lovers, each one evil spoken of;
O smitten lips wherethrough this voice of mine
Came softer with her praise;
Abide a little for our lady's love.
The kisses of her mouth were more than wine,
And more than peace the passage of her days.

O Love, thou knowest if she were good to see.
O Time, thou shalt not find in any land
Till, cast out of thine hand,
The sunlight and the moonlight fail from thee,
Another woman fashioned like as this.
O Sin, thou knowest that all thy shame in her
Was made a goodly thing;
Yea, she caught Shame and shamed him with her kiss,
With her fair kiss, and lips much lovelier
Than lips of amorous roses in late spring.

By night there stood over against my bed

Queen Venus with a hood striped gold and black,
Both sides drawn fully back
From brows wherein the sad blood failed of red,
And temples drained of purple and full of death.
Her curled hair had the wave of sea-water
And the sea's gold in it.
Her eyes were as a dove's that sickeneth.
Strewn dust of gold she had shed over her,
And pearl and purple and amber on her feet.

Upon her raiment of dyed sendaline
Were painted all the secret ways of love
And covered things thereof,
That hold delight as grape-flowers hold their wine;
Red mouths of maidens and red feet of doves,
And brides that kept within the bride-chamber
Their garment of soft shame,
And weeping faces of the wearied loves
That swoon in sleep and awake wearier,
With heat of lips and hair shed out like flame.

The tears that through her eyelids fell on me
Made mine own bitter where they ran between
As blood had fallen therein,
She saying; Arise, lift up thine eyes and see
If any glad thing be or any good
Now the best thing is taken forth of us;
Even she to whom all praise
Was as one flower in a great multitude,
One glorious flower of many and glorious,
One day found gracious among many days:

Even she whose handmaiden was Love--to whom
At kissing times across her stateliest bed
Kings bowed themselves and shed
Pale wine, and honey with the honeycomb,

And spikenard bruised for a burnt-offering;
Even she between whose lips the kiss became
As fire and frankincense;
Whose hair was as gold raiment on a king,
Whose eyes were as the morning purged with flame,
Whose eyelids as sweet savour issuing thence.

Then I beheld, and lo on the other side
My lady's likeness crowned and robed and dead.
Sweet still, but now not red,
Was the shut mouth whereby men lived and died.
And sweet, but emptied of the blood's blue shade,
The great curled eyelids that withheld her eyes.
And sweet, but like spoilt gold,
The weight of colour in her tresses weighed.
And sweet, but as a vesture with new dyes,
The body that was clothed with love of old.

Ah! that my tears filled all her woven hair
And all the hollow bosom of her gown--
Ah! that my tears ran down
Even to the place where many kisses were,
Even where her parted breast-flowers have place,
Even where they are cloven apart--who knows not this?
Ah! the flowers cleave apart
And their sweet fills the tender interspace;
Ah! the leaves grown thereof were things to kiss
Ere their fine gold was tarnished at the heart.

Ah! in the days when God did good to me,
Each part about her was a righteous thing;
Her mouth an almsgiving,
The glory of her garments charity,
The beauty of her bosom a good deed,
In the good days when God kept sight of us;
Love lay upon her eyes,

And on that hair whereof the world takes heed;
And all her body was more virtuous
Than souls of women fashioned otherwise.

Now, ballad, gather poppies in thine hands
And sheaves of brier and many rusted sheaves
Rain-rotten in rank lands,
Waste marigold and late unhappy leaves
And grass that fades ere any of it be mown;
And when thy bosom is filled full thereof
Seek out Death's face ere the light altereth,
And say "My master that was thrall to Love
Is become thrall to Death."
Bow down before him, ballad, sigh and groan,
But make no sojourn in thy outgoing;
For haply it may be
That when thy feet return at evening
Death shall come in with thee.

LAUS VENERIS

Lors dit en plourant; Helas trop malheureux homme et mauldict pescheur, oncques ne verrai-je clemence et misericorde de Dieu. Ores m'en irai-je d'icy et me cacherai dedans le mont Horsel, en requerant de faveur et d'amoureuse merci ma doulce dame Venus, car pour son amour serai-je bien a tout jamais damne en enfer. Voicy la fin de tous mes faicts d'armes et de toutes mes belles chansons. Helas, trop belle estoyt la face de ma dame et ses yeulx, et en mauvais jour je vis ces chouses-la. Lors s'en alla tout en gemissant et se retourna chez elle, et la vescut tristement en grand amour pres de sa dame. Puis apres advint que le pape vit un jour esclater sur son baston force belles fleurs rouges et blanches et maints boutons de feuilles, et ainsi vit-il reverdir toute l'escorce. Ce dont il eut grande crainte et moult s'en esmut, et grande pitie lui prit de ce chevalier qui s'en estoyt departi sans espoir comme un homme miserable et damne. Doncques envoya force messaigers devers luy pour le ramener, disant qu'il aurait de Dieu grace et bonne absolution de son grand pesche d'amour. Mais oncques plus ne le virent; car toujours demeura ce pauvre chevalier aupres de Venus la haulte et forte deesse es flancs de la montagne amoureuse.

Livre des grandes merveilles d'amour, escript en latin et en francoys par Maistre Antoine Gaget._ 1530.

LAUS VENERIS

Asleep or waking is it? for her neck,
Kissed over close, wears yet a purple speck
   Wherein the pained blood falters and goes out;
Soft, and stung softly--fairer for a fleck.

But though my lips shut sucking on the place,
There is no vein at work upon her face;
   Her eyelids are so peaceable, no doubt
Deep sleep has warmed her blood through all its ways.

Lo, this is she that was the world's delight;
The old grey years were parcels of her might;
   The strewings of the ways wherein she trod
Were the twain seasons of the day and night.

Lo, she was thus when her clear limbs enticed
All lips that now grow sad with kissing Christ,
   Stained with blood fallen from the feet of God,
The feet and hands whereat our souls were priced.

Alas, Lord, surely thou art great and fair.
But lo her wonderfully woven hair!
   And thou didst heal us with thy piteous kiss;
But see now, Lord; her mouth is lovelier.

She is right fair; what hath she done to thee?
Nay, fair Lord Christ, lift up thine eyes and see;
   Had now thy mother such a lip--like this?
Thou knowest how sweet a thing it is to me.

Inside the Horsel here the air is hot;
Right little peace one hath for it, God wot;
   The scented dusty daylight burns the air,
And my heart chokes me till I hear it not.

Behold, my Venus, my soul's body, lies
With my love laid upon her garment-wise,
  Feeling my love in all her limbs and hair
And shed between her eyelids through her eyes.

She holds my heart in her sweet open hands
Hanging asleep; hard by her head there stands,
  Crowned with gilt thorns and clothed with flesh like fire,
Love, wan as foam blown up the salt burnt sands--

Hot as the brackish waifs of yellow spume
That shift and steam--loose clots of arid fume
  From the sea's panting mouth of dry desire;
There stands he, like one labouring at a loom.

The warp holds fast across; and every thread
That makes the woof up has dry specks of red;
  Always the shuttle cleaves clean through, and he
Weaves with the hair of many a ruined head.

Love is not glad nor sorry, as I deem;
Labouring he dreams, and labours in the dream,
  Till when the spool is finished, lo I see
His web, reeled off, curls and goes out like steam.

Night falls like fire; the heavy lights run low,
And as they drop, my blood and body so
  Shake as the flame shakes, full of days and hours
That sleep not neither weep they as they go.

Ah yet would God this flesh of mine might be
Where air might wash and long leaves cover me,
  Where tides of grass break into foam of flowers,
Or where the wind's feet shine along the sea.

Ah yet would God that stems and roots were bred
Out of my weary body and my head,
  That sleep were sealed upon me with a seal,
And I were as the least of all his dead.

Would God my blood were dew to feed the grass,
Mine ears made deaf and mine eyes blind as glass,
  My body broken as a turning wheel,
And my mouth stricken ere it saith Alas!

Ah God, that love were as a flower or flame,
That life were as the naming of a name,
  That death were not more pitiful than desire,
That these things were not one thing and the same!

Behold now, surely somewhere there is death:
For each man hath some space of years, he saith,
  A little space of time ere time expire,
A little day, a little way of breath.

And lo, between the sundawn and the sun,
His day's work and his night's work are undone;
  And lo, between the nightfall and the light,
He is not, and none knoweth of such an one.

Ah God, that I were as all souls that be,
As any herb or leaf of any tree,
  As men that toil through hours of labouring night,
As bones of men under the deep sharp sea.

Outside it must be winter among men;
For at the gold bars of the gates again
  I heard all night and all the hours of it
The wind's wet wings and fingers drip with rain.

Knights gather, riding sharp for cold; I know

The ways and woods are strangled with the snow;
  And with short song the maidens spin and sit
Until Christ's birthnight, lily-like, arow.

The scent and shadow shed about me make
The very soul in all my senses ache;
  The hot hard night is fed upon my breath,
And sleep beholds me from afar awake.

Alas, but surely where the hills grow deep,
Or where the wild ways of the sea are steep,
  Or in strange places somewhere there is death,
And on death's face the scattered hair of sleep.

There lover-like with lips and limbs that meet
They lie, they pluck sweet fruit of life and eat;
  But me the hot and hungry days devour,
And in my mouth no fruit of theirs is sweet.

No fruit of theirs, but fruit of my desire,
For her love's sake whose lips through mine respire;
  Her eyelids on her eyes like flower on flower,
Mine eyelids on mine eyes like fire on fire.

So lie we, not as sleep that lies by death,
With heavy kisses and with happy breath;
  Not as man lies by woman, when the bride
Laughs low for love's sake and the words he saith.

For she lies, laughing low with love; she lies
And turns his kisses on her lips to sighs,
  To sighing sound of lips unsatisfied,
And the sweet tears are tender with her eyes.

Ah, not as they, but as the souls that were
Slain in the old time, having found her fair;

Who, sleeping with her lips upon their eyes,
Heard sudden serpents hiss across her hair.

Their blood runs round the roots of time like rain:
She casts them forth and gathers them again;
   With nerve and bone she weaves and multiplies
Exceeding pleasure out of extreme pain.

Her little chambers drip with flower-like red,
Her girdles, and the chaplets of her head,
   Her armlets and her anklets; with her feet
She tramples all that winepress of the dead.

Her gateways smoke with fume of flowers and fires,
With loves burnt out and unassuaged desires;
   Between her lips the steam of them is sweet,
The languor in her ears of many lyres.

Her beds are full of perfume and sad sound,
Her doors are made with music, and barred round
   With sighing and with laughter and with tears,
With tears whereby strong souls of men are bound.

There is the knight Adonis that was slain;
With flesh and blood she chains him for a chain;
   The body and the spirit in her ears
Cry, for her lips divide him vein by vein.

Yea, all she slayeth; yea, every man save me;
Me, love, thy lover that must cleave to thee
   Till the ending of the days and ways of earth,
The shaking of the sources of the sea.

Me, most forsaken of all souls that fell;
Me, satiated with things insatiable;
   Me, for whose sake the extreme hell makes mirth,

Yea, laughter kindles at the heart of hell.

Alas thy beauty! for thy mouth's sweet sake
My soul is bitter to me, my limbs quake
  As water, as the flesh of men that weep,
As their heart's vein whose heart goes nigh to break.

Ah God, that sleep with flower-sweet finger-tips
Would crush the fruit of death upon my lips;
  Ah God, that death would tread the grapes of sleep
And wring their juice upon me as it drips.

There is no change of cheer for many days,
But change of chimes high up in the air, that sways
  Rung by the running fingers of the wind;
And singing sorrows heard on hidden ways.

Day smiteth day in twain, night sundereth night,
And on mine eyes the dark sits as the light;
  Yea, Lord, thou knowest I know not, having sinned,
If heaven be clean or unclean in thy sight.

Yea, as if earth were sprinkled over me,
Such chafed harsh earth as chokes a sandy sea,
  Each pore doth yearn, and the dried blood thereof
Gasps by sick fits, my heart swims heavily,

There is a feverish famine in my veins;
Below her bosom, where a crushed grape stains
  The white and blue, there my lips caught and clove
An hour since, and what mark of me remains?

I dare not always touch her, lest the kiss
Leave my lips charred. Yea, Lord, a little bliss,
  Brief bitter bliss, one hath for a great sin;
Nathless thou knowest how sweet a thing it is.

Sin, is it sin whereby men's souls are thrust
Into the pit? yet had I a good trust
　To save my soul before it slipped therein,
Trod under by the fire-shod feet of lust.

For if mine eyes fail and my soul takes breath,
I look between the iron sides of death
　Into sad hell where all sweet love hath end,
All but the pain that never finisheth.

There are the naked faces of great kings,
The singing folk with all their lute-playings;
　There when one cometh he shall have to friend
The grave that covets and the worm that clings.

There sit the knights that were so great of hand,
The ladies that were queens of fair green land,
　Grown grey and black now, brought unto the dust,
Soiled, without raiment, clad about with sand.

There is one end for all of them; they sit
Naked and sad, they drink the dregs of it,
　Trodden as grapes in the wine-press of lust.
Trampled and trodden by the fiery feet.

I see the marvelous mouth whereby there fell
Cities and people whom the gods loved well,
　Yet for her sake on them the fire gat hold,
And for their sakes on her the fire of hell.

And softer than the Egyptian lote-leaf is,
The queen whose face was worth the world to kiss,
　Wearing at breast a suckling snake of gold;
And large pale lips of strong Semiramis,

Curled like a tiger's that curl back to feed;
Red only where the last kiss made them bleed;
  Her hair most thick with many a carven gem,
Deep in the mane, great-chested, like a steed.

Yea, with red sin the faces of them shine;
But in all these there was no sin like mine;
  No, not in all the strange great sins of them
That made the wine-press froth and foam with wine.

For I was of Christ's choosing, I God's knight,
No blinkard heathen stumbling for scant light;
  I can well see, for all the dusty days
Gone past, the clean great time of goodly fight.

I smell the breathing battle sharp with blows,
With shriek of shafts and snapping short of bows;
  The fair pure sword smites out in subtle ways,
Sounds and long lights are shed between the rows

Of beautiful mailed men; the edged light slips,
Most like a snake that takes short breath and dips
  Sharp from the beautifully bending head,
With all its gracious body lithe as lips

That curl in touching you; right in this wise
My sword doth, seeming fire in mine own eyes,
  Leaving all colours in them brown and red
And flecked with death; then the keen breaths like sighs,

The caught-up choked dry laughters following them,
When all the fighting face is grown a flame
  For pleasure, and the pulse that stuns the ears,
And the heart's gladness of the goodly game.

Let me think yet a little; I do know

These things were sweet, but sweet such years ago,
  Their savour is all turned now into tears;
Yea, ten years since, where the blue ripples blow,

The blue curled eddies of the blowing Rhine,
I felt the sharp wind shaking grass and vine
  Touch my blood too, and sting me with delight
Through all this waste and weary body of mine

That never feels clear air; right gladly then
I rode alone, a great way off my men,
  And heard the chiming bridle smite and smite,
And gave each rhyme thereof some rhyme again,

Till my song shifted to that iron one;
Seeing there rode up between me and the sun
  Some certain of my foe's men, for his three
White wolves across their painted coats did run.

The first red-bearded, with square cheeks--alack,
I made my knave's blood turn his beard to black;
  The slaying of him was a joy to see:
Perchance too, when at night he came not back,

Some woman fell a-weeping, whom this thief
Would beat when he had drunken; yet small grief
  Hath any for the ridding of such knaves;
Yea, if one wept, I doubt her teen was brief.

This bitter love is sorrow in all lands,
Draining of eyelids, wringing of drenched hands,
  Sighing of hearts and filling up of graves;
A sign across the head of the world he stands,

An one that hath a plague-mark on his brows;
Dust and spilt blood do track him to his house

  Down under earth; sweet smells of lip and cheek,
Like a sweet snake's breath made more poisonous

With chewing of some perfumed deadly grass,
Are shed all round his passage if he pass,
  And their quenched savour leaves the whole soul weak,
Sick with keen guessing whence the perfume was.

As one who hidden in deep sedge and reeds
Smells the rare scent made where a panther feeds,
  And tracking ever slotwise the warm smell
Is snapped upon by the sweet mouth and bleeds,

His head far down the hot sweet throat of her--
So one tracks love, whose breath is deadlier,
  And lo, one springe and you are fast in hell,
Fast as the gin's grip of a wayfarer.

I think now, as the heavy hours decease
One after one, and bitter thoughts increase
  One upon one, of all sweet finished things;
The breaking of the battle; the long peace

Wherein we sat clothed softly, each man's hair
Crowned with green leaves beneath white hoods of vair;
  The sounds of sharp spears at great tourneyings,
And noise of singing in the late sweet air.

I sang of love too, knowing nought thereof;
"Sweeter," I said, "the little laugh of love
  Than tears out of the eyes of Magdalen,
Or any fallen feather of the Dove.

"The broken little laugh that spoils a kiss,
The ache of purple pulses, and the bliss
  Of blinded eyelids that expand again--

Love draws them open with those lips of his,

"Lips that cling hard till the kissed face has grown
Of one same fire and colour with their own;
  Then ere one sleep, appeased with sacrifice,
Where his lips wounded, there his lips atone."

I sang these things long since and knew them not;
"Lo, here is love, or there is love, God wot,
  This man and that finds favour in his eyes,"
I said, "but I, what guerdon have I got?

"The dust of praise that is blown everywhere
In all men's faces with the common air;
  The bay-leaf that wants chafing to be sweet
Before they wind it in a singer's hair."

So that one dawn I rode forth sorrowing;
I had no hope but of some evil thing,
  And so rode slowly past the windy wheat
And past the vineyard and the water-spring,

Up to the Horsel. A great elder-tree
Held back its heaps of flowers to let me see
  The ripe tall grass, and one that walked therein,
Naked, with hair shed over to the knee.

She walked between the blossom and the grass;
I knew the beauty of her, what she was,
  The beauty of her body and her sin,
And in my flesh the sin of hers, alas!

Alas! for sorrow is all the end of this.
O sad kissed mouth, how sorrowful it is!
  O breast whereat some suckling sorrow clings,
Red with the bitter blossom of a kiss!

Ah, with blind lips I felt for you, and found
About my neck your hands and hair enwound,
  The hands that stifle and the hair that stings,
I felt them fasten sharply without sound.

Yea, for my sin I had great store of bliss:
Rise up, make answer for me, let thy kiss
  Seal my lips hard from speaking of my sin,
Lest one go mad to hear how sweet it is.

Yet I waxed faint with fume of barren bowers,
And murmuring of the heavy-headed hours;
  And let the dove's beak fret and peck within
My lips in vain, and Love shed fruitless flowers.

So that God looked upon me when your hands
Were hot about me; yea, God brake my bands
  To save my soul alive, and I came forth
Like a man blind and naked in strange lands

That hears men laugh and weep, and knows not whence
Nor wherefore, but is broken in his sense;
  Howbeit I met folk riding from the north
Towards Rome, to purge them of their souls' offense,

And rode with them, and spake to none; the day
Stunned me like lights upon some wizard way,
  And ate like fire mine eyes and mine eyesight;
So rode I, hearing all these chant and pray,

And marvelled; till before us rose and fell
White cursed hills, like outer skirts of hell
  Seen where men's eyes look through the day to night,
Like a jagged shell's lips, harsh, untunable,

Blown in between by devils' wrangling breath;
Nathless we won well past that hell and death,
   Down to the sweet land where all airs are good,
Even unto Rome where God's grace tarrieth.

Then came each man and worshipped at his knees
Who in the Lord God's likeness bears the keys
   To bind or loose, and called on Christ's shed blood,
And so the sweet-souled father gave him ease.

But when I came I fell down at his feet,
Saying, "Father, though the Lord's blood be right sweet,
   The spot it takes not off the panther's skin,
Nor shall an Ethiop's stain be bleached with it.

"Lo, I have sinned and have spat out at God,
Wherefore his hand is heavier and his rod
   More sharp because of mine exceeding sin,
And all his raiment redder than bright blood

"Before mine eyes; yea, for my sake I wot
The heat of hell is waxen seven times hot
   Through my great sin." Then spake he some sweet word,
Giving me cheer; which thing availed me not;

Yea, scarce I wist if such indeed were said;
For when I ceased--lo, as one newly dead
   Who hears a great cry out of hell, I heard
The crying of his voice across my head.

"Until this dry shred staff, that hath no whit
Of leaf nor bark, bear blossom and smell sweet,
   Seek thou not any mercy in God's sight,
For so long shalt thou be cast out from it."

Yea, what if dried-up stems wax red and green,

Shall that thing be which is not nor has been?
  Yea, what if sapless bark wax green and white,
Shall any good fruit grow upon my sin?

Nay, though sweet fruit were plucked of a dry tree,
And though men drew sweet waters of the sea,
  There should not grow sweet leaves on this dead stem,
This waste wan body and shaken soul of me.

Yea, though God search it warily enough,
There is not one sound thing in all thereof;
  Though he search all my veins through, searching them
He shall find nothing whole therein but love.

For I came home right heavy, with small cheer,
And lo my love, mine own soul's heart, more dear
  Than mine own soul, more beautiful than God,
Who hath my being between the hands of her--

Fair still, but fair for no man saving me,
As when she came out of the naked sea
  Making the foam as fire whereon she trod,
And as the inner flower of fire was she.

Yea, she laid hold upon me, and her mouth
Clove unto mine as soul to body doth,
  And, laughing, made her lips luxurious;
Her hair had smells of all the sunburnt south,

Strange spice and flower, strange savour of crushed fruit,
And perfume the swart kings tread underfoot
  For pleasure when their minds wax amorous,
Charred frankincense and grated sandal-root.

And I forgot fear and all weary things,
All ended prayers and perished thanksgivings,

Feeling her face with all her eager hair
Cleave to me, clinging as a fire that clings

To the body and to the raiment, burning them;
As after death I know that such-like flame
   Shall cleave to me for ever; yea, what care,
Albeit I burn then, having felt the same?

Ah love, there is no better life than this;
To have known love, how bitter a thing it is,
   And afterward be cast out of God's sight;
Yea, these that know not, shall they have such bliss

High up in barren heaven before his face
As we twain in the heavy-hearted place,
   Remembering love and all the dead delight,
And all that time was sweet with for a space?

For till the thunder in the trumpet be,
Soul may divide from body, but not we
   One from another; I hold thee with my hand,
I let mine eyes have all their will of thee,

I seal myself upon thee with my might,
Abiding alway out of all men's sight
   Until God loosen over sea and land
The thunder of the trumpets of the night.

EXPLICIT LAUS VENERIS

PHÆDRA

HIPPOLYTUS; PHÆDRA; CHORUS OF TROEZENIAN WOMEN

HIPPOLYTUS.

Lay not thine hand upon me; let me go;
Take off thine eyes that put the gods to shame;
What, wilt thou turn my loathing to thy death?

PHÆDRA.

Nay, I will never loosen hold nor breathe
Till thou have slain me; godlike for great brows
Thou art, and thewed as gods are, with clear hair:
Draw now thy sword and smite me as thou art god,
For verily I am smitten of other gods,
Why not of thee?

CHORUS.

O queen, take heed of words;
Why wilt thou eat the husk of evil speech?
Wear wisdom for that veil about thy head
And goodness for the binding of thy brows.

PHÆDRA.

Nay, but this god hath cause enow to smite;
If he will slay me, baring breast and throat,

I lean toward the stroke with silent mouth
And a great heart. Come, take thy sword and slay;
Let me not starve between desire and death,
But send me on my way with glad wet lips;
For in the vein-drawn ashen-coloured palm
Death's hollow hand holds water of sweet draught
To dip and slake dried mouths at, as a deer
Specked red from thorns laps deep and loses pain.
Yea, if mine own blood ran upon my mouth,
I would drink that. Nay, but be swift with me;
Set thy sword here between the girdle and breast,
For I shall grow a poison if I live.
Are not my cheeks as grass, my body pale,
And my breath like a dying poisoned man's?
O whatsoever of godlike names thou be,
By thy chief name I charge thee, thou strong god,
And bid thee slay me. Strike, up to the gold,
Up to the hand-grip of the hilt; strike here;
For I am Cretan of my birth; strike now;
For I am Theseus' wife; stab up to the rims,
I am born daughter to Pasiphae.
See thou spare not for greatness of my blood,
Nor for the shining letters of my name:
Make thy sword sure inside thine hand and smite,
For the bright writing of my name is black,
And I am sick with hating the sweet sun.

HIPPOLYTUS.

Let not this woman wail and cleave to me,
That am no part of the gods' wrath with her;
Loose ye her hands from me lest she take hurt.

CHORUS.

Lady, this speech and majesty are twain;
Pure shame is of one counsel with the gods.

HIPPOLYTUS.

Man is as beast when shame stands off from him.

PHÆDRA.

Man, what have I to do with shame or thee?
I am not of one counsel with the gods.
I am their kin, I have strange blood in me,
I am not of their likeness nor of thine:
My veins are mixed, and therefore am I mad,
Yea therefore chafe and turn on mine own flesh,
Half of a woman made with half a god.
But thou wast hewn out of an iron womb
And fed with molten mother-snow for milk.
A sword was nurse of thine; Hippolyta,
That had the spear to father, and the axe
To bridesman, and wet blood of sword-slain men
For wedding-water out of a noble well,
Even she did bear thee, thinking of a sword,
And thou wast made a man mistakingly.
Nay, for I love thee, I will have thy hands,
Nay, for I will not loose thee, thou art sweet,
Thou art my son, I am thy father's wife,
I ache toward thee with a bridal blood,
The pulse is heavy in all my married veins,
My whole face beats, I will feed full of thee,
My body is empty of ease, I will be fed,
I am burnt to the bone with love, thou shalt not go,
I am heartsick, and mine eyelids prick mine eyes,
Thou shalt not sleep nor eat nor say a word
Till thou hast slain me. I am not good to live.

CHORUS.

This is an evil born with all its teeth,
When love is cast out of the bound of love.

HIPPOLYTUS.

There is no hate that is so hateworthy.

PHÆDRA.

I pray thee turn that hate of thine my way,
I hate not it nor anything of thine.
Lo, maidens, how he burns about the brow,
And draws the chafing sword-strap down his hand.
What wilt thou do? wilt thou be worse than death?
Be but as sweet as is the bitterest,
The most dispiteous out of all the gods,
I am well pleased. Lo, do I crave so much?
I do but bid thee be unmerciful,
Even the one thing thou art. Pity me not:
Thou wert not quick to pity. Think of me
As of a thing thy hounds are keen upon
In the wet woods between the windy ways,
And slay me for a spoil. This body of mine
Is worth a wild beast's fell or hide of hair,
And spotted deeper than a panther's grain.
I were but dead if thou wert pure indeed;
I pray thee by thy cold green holy crown
And by the fillet-leaves of Artemis.
Nay, but thou wilt not. Death is not like thee.
Albeit men hold him worst of all the gods.
For of all gods Death only loves not gifts,
Nor with burnt-offering nor blood-sacrifice
Shalt thou do aught to get thee grace of him;
He will have nought of altar and altar-song,

And from him only of all the lords in heaven
Persuasion turns a sweet averted mouth.
But thou art worse: from thee with baffled breath
Back on my lips my prayer falls like a blow,
And beats upon them, dumb. What shall I say?
There is no word I can compel thee with
To do me good and slay me. But take heed;
I say, be wary; look between thy feet,
Lest a snare take them though the ground be good.

HIPPOLYTUS.

Shame may do most where fear is found most weak;
That which for shame's sake yet I have not done,
Shall it be done for fear's? Take thine own way;
Better the foot slip than the whole soul swerve.

PHÆDRA.

The man is choice and exquisite of mouth;
Yet in the end a curse shall curdle it.

CHORUS.

He goes with cloak upgathered to the lip,
Holding his eye as with some ill in sight.

PHÆDRA.

A bitter ill he hath i' the way thereof,
And it shall burn the sight out as with fire.

CHORUS.

Speak no such word whereto mischance is kin.

PHÆDRA.

Out of my heart and by fate's leave I speak.

CHORUS.

Set not thy heart to follow after fate.

PHÆDRA.

O women, O sweet people of this land,
O goodly city and pleasant ways thereof,
And woods with pasturing grass and great well-heads,
And hills with light and night between your leaves,
And winds with sound and silence in your lips,
And earth and water and all immortal things,
I take you to my witness what I am.
There is a god about me like as fire,
Sprung whence, who knoweth, or who hath heart to say?
A god more strong than whom slain beasts can soothe,
Or honey, or any spilth of blood-like wine,
Nor shall one please him with a whitened brow
Nor wheat nor wool nor aught of plaited leaf.
For like my mother am I stung and slain,
And round my cheeks have such red malady
And on my lips such fire and foam as hers.
This is that Ate out of Amathus
That breeds up death and gives it one for love.
She hath slain mercy, and for dead mercy's sake
(Being frighted with this sister that was slain)
Flees from before her fearful-footed shame,
And will not bear the bending of her brows
And long soft arrows flown from under them
As from bows bent. Desire flows out of her
As out of lips doth speech: and over her
Shines fire, and round her and beneath her fire.

She hath sown pain and plague in all our house,
Love loathed of love, and mates unmatchable,
Wild wedlock, and the lusts that bleat or low,
And marriage-fodder snuffed about of kine.
Lo how the heifer runs with leaping flank
Sleek under shaggy and speckled lies of hair,
And chews a horrible lip, and with harsh tongue
Laps alien froth and licks a loathlier mouth.
Alas, a foul first steam of trodden tares,
And fouler of these late grapes underfoot.
A bitter way of waves and clean-cut foam
Over the sad road of sonorous sea
The high gods gave king Theseus for no love,
Nay, but for love, yet to no loving end.
Alas the long thwarts and the fervent oars,
And blown hard sails that straightened the scant rope!
There were no strong pools in the hollow sea
To drag at them and suck down side and beak,
No wind to catch them in the teeth and hair,
No shoal, no shallow among the roaring reefs,
No gulf whereout the straining tides throw spars,
No surf where white bones twist like whirled white fire.
But like to death he came with death, and sought
And slew and spoiled and gat him that he would.
For death, for marriage, and for child-getting,
I set my curse against him as a sword;
Yea, and the severed half thereof I leave
Pittheus, because he slew not (when that face
Was tender, and the life still soft in it)
The small swathed child, but bred him for my fate.
I would I had been the first that took her death
Out from between wet hoofs and reddened teeth,
Splashed horns, fierce fetlocks of the brother bull?
For now shall I take death a deadlier way,
Gathering it up between the feet of love
Or off the knees of murder reaching it.

THE TRIUMPH OF TIME

Before our lives divide forever,
  While time is with us and hands are free,
(Time, swift to fasten and swift to sever
  Hand from hand, as we stand by the sea)
I will say no word that a man might say
Whose whole life's love goes down in a day;
For this could never have been; and never,
  Though the gods and the years relent, shall be.

Is it worth a tear, is it worth an hour,
  To think of things that are well outworn?
Of fruitless husk and fugitive flower,
  The dream foregone and the deed forborne?
Though joy be done with and grief be vain,
Time shall not sever us wholly in twain;
Earth is not spoilt for a single shower;
  But the rain has ruined the ungrown corn.

It will grow not again, this fruit of my heart,
  Smitten with sunbeams, ruined with rain.
The singing seasons divide and depart,
  Winter and summer depart in twain.
It will grow not again, it is ruined at root,
The bloodlike blossom, the dull red fruit;
Though the heart yet sickens, the lips yet smart,
  With sullen savour of poisonous pain.

I have given no man of my fruit to eat;
  I trod the grapes, I have drunken the wine.
Had you eaten and drunken and found it sweet,
  This wild new growth of the corn and vine,
This wine and bread without lees or leaven,
We had grown as gods, as the gods in heaven,

Souls fair to look upon, goodly to greet,
  One splendid spirit, your soul and mine.

In the change of years, in the coil of things,
  In the clamour and rumour of life to be,
We, drinking love at the furthest springs,
  Covered with love as a covering tree,
We had grown as gods, as the gods above,
Filled from the heart to the lips with love,
Held fast in his hands, clothed warm with his wings,
  O love, my love, had you loved but me!

We had stood as the sure stars stand, and moved
  As the moon moves, loving the world; and seen
Grief collapse as a thing disproved,
  Death consume as a thing unclean.
Twain halves of a perfect heart, made fast
Soul to soul while the years fell past;
Had you loved me once, as you have not loved;
  Had the chance been with us that has not been.

I have put my days and dreams out of mind,
  Days that are over, dreams that are done.
Though we seek life through, we shall surely find
  There is none of them clear to us now, not one.
But clear are these things; the grass and the sand,
Where, sure as the eyes reach, ever at hand,
With lips wide open and face burnt blind,
  The strong sea-daisies feast on the sun.

The low downs lean to the sea; the stream,
  One loose thin pulseless tremulous vein,
Rapid and vivid and dumb as a dream,
  Works downward, sick of the sun and the rain;
No wind is rough with the rank rare flowers;
The sweet sea, mother of loves and hours,

Shudders and shines as the grey winds gleam,
  Turning her smile to a fugitive pain.

Mother of loves that are swift to fade,
  Mother of mutable winds and hours.
A barren mother, a mother-maid,
  Cold and clean as her faint salt flowers.
I would we twain were even as she,
Lost in the night and the light of the sea,
Where faint sounds falter and wan beams wade,
  Break, and are broken, and shed into showers.

The loves and hours of the life of a man,
  They are swift and sad, being born of the sea.
Hours that rejoice and regret for a span,
  Born with a man's breath, mortal as he;
Loves that are lost ere they come to birth,
Weeds of the wave, without fruit upon earth.
I lose what I long for, save what I can,
  My love, my love, and no love for me!

It is not much that a man can save
  On the sands of life, in the straits of time,
Who swims in sight of the great third wave
  That never a swimmer shall cross or climb.
Some waif washed up with the strays and spars
That ebb-tide shows to the shore and the stars;
Weed from the water, grass from a grave,
  A broken blossom, a ruined rhyme.

There will no man do for your sake, I think,
  What I would have done for the least word said.
I had wrung life dry for your lips to drink,
  Broken it up for your daily bread:
Body for body and blood for blood,
As the flow of the full sea risen to flood

That yearns and trembles before it sink,
  I had given, and lain down for you, glad and dead.

Yea, hope at highest and all her fruit,
  And time at fullest and all his dower,
I had given you surely, and life to boot,
  Were we once made one for a single hour.
But now, you are twain, you are cloven apart,
Flesh of his flesh, but heart of my heart;
And deep in one is the bitter root,
  And sweet for one is the lifelong flower.

To have died if you cared I should die for you, clung
  To my life if you bade me, played my part
As it pleased you--these were the thoughts that stung,
  The dreams that smote with a keener dart
Than shafts of love or arrows of death;
These were but as fire is, dust, or breath,
Or poisonous foam on the tender tongue
  Of the little snakes that eat my heart.

I wish we were dead together to-day,
  Lost sight of, hidden away out of sight,
Clasped and clothed in the cloven clay,
  Out of the world's way, out of the light,
Out of the ages of worldly weather,
Forgotten of all men altogether,
As the world's first dead, taken wholly away,
  Made one with death, filled full of the night.

How we should slumber, how we should sleep,
  Far in the dark with the dreams and the dews!
And dreaming, grow to each other, and weep,
  Laugh low, live softly, murmur and muse;
Yea, and it may be, struck through by the dream,

Feel the dust quicken and quiver, and seem
Alive as of old to the lips, and leap
  Spirit to spirit as lovers use.

Sick dreams and sad of a dull delight;
  For what shall it profit when men are dead
To have dreamed, to have loved with the whole soul's might,
  To have looked for day when the day was fled?
Let come what will, there is one thing worth,
To have had fair love in the life upon earth:
To have held love safe till the day grew night,
  While skies had colour and lips were red.

Would I lose you now? would I take you then,
  If I lose you now that my heart has need?
And come what may after death to men,
  What thing worth this will the dead years breed?
Lose life, lose all; but at least I know,
O sweet life's love, having loved you so,
Had I reached you on earth, I should lose not again,
  In death nor life, nor in dream or deed.

Yea, I know this well: were you once sealed mine,
  Mine in the blood's beat, mine in the breath,
Mixed into me as honey in wine,
  Not time, that sayeth and gainsayeth,
Nor all strong things had severed us then;
Not wrath of gods, nor wisdom of men,
Nor all things earthly, nor all divine,
  Nor joy nor sorrow, nor life nor death.
I had grown pure as the dawn and the dew,
  You had grown strong as the sun or the sea.
But none shall triumph a whole life through:
  For death is one, and the fates are three.
At the door of life, by the gate of breath,

There are worse things waiting for men than death;
Death could not sever my soul and you,
  As these have severed your soul from me.

You have chosen and clung to the chance they sent you,
  Life sweet as perfume and pure as prayer.
But will it not one day in heaven repent you?
  Will they solace you wholly, the days that were?
Will you lift up your eyes between sadness and bliss,
Meet mine, and see where the great love is,
And tremble and turn and be changed? Content you;
  The gate is strait; I shall not be there.

But you, had you chosen, had you stretched hand,
  Had you seen good such a thing were done,
I too might have stood with the souls that stand
  In the sun's sight, clothed with the light of the sun;
But who now on earth need care how I live?
Have the high gods anything left to give,
Save dust and laurels and gold and sand?
  Which gifts are goodly; but I will none.

O all fair lovers about the world,
  There is none of you, none, that shall comfort me.
My thoughts are as dead things, wrecked and whirled
  Round and round in a gulf of the sea;
And still, through the sound and the straining stream,
Through the coil and chafe, they gleam in a dream,
The bright fine lips so cruelly curled,
  And strange swift eyes where the soul sits free.
Free, without pity, withheld from woe,
  Ignorant; fair as the eyes are fair.
Would I have you change now, change at a blow,
  Startled and stricken, awake and aware?
Yea, if I could, would I have you see
My very love of you filling me,

And know my soul to the quick, as I know
  The likeness and look of your throat and hair?

I shall not change you. Nay, though I might,
  Would I change my sweet one love with a word?
I had rather your hair should change in a night,
  Clear now as the plume of a black bright bird;
Your face fail suddenly, cease, turn grey,
Die as a leaf that dies in a day.
I will keep my soul in a place out of sight,
  Far off, where the pulse of it is not heard.

Far off it walks, in a bleak blown space,
  Full of the sound of the sorrow of years.
I have woven a veil for the weeping face,
  Whose lips have drunken the wine of tears;
I have found a way for the failing feet,
A place for slumber and sorrow to meet;
There is no rumour about the place,
  Nor light, nor any that sees or hears.

I have hidden my soul out of sight, and said
  "Let none take pity upon thee, none
Comfort thy crying: for lo, thou art dead,
  Lie still now, safe out of sight of the sun.
Have I not built thee a grave, and wrought
Thy grave-clothes on thee of grievous thought,
With soft spun verses and tears unshed,
  And sweet light visions of things undone?
"I have given thee garments and balm and myrrh,
  And gold, and beautiful burial things.
But thou, be at peace now, make no stir;
  Is not thy grave as a royal king's?
Fret not thyself though the end were sore;
Sleep, be patient, vex me no more.
Sleep; what hast thou to do with her?

The eyes that weep, with the mouth that sings?"

Where the dead red leaves of the years lie rotten,
  The cold old crimes and the deeds thrown by,
The misconceived and the misbegotten,
  I would find a sin to do ere I die,
Sure to dissolve and destroy me all through,
That would set you higher in heaven, serve you
And leave you happy, when clean forgotten,
  As a dead man out of mind, am I.

Your lithe hands draw me, your face burns through me,
  I am swift to follow you, keen to see;
But love lacks might to redeem or undo me;
  As I have been, I know I shall surely be;
"What should such fellows as I do?" Nay,
My part were worse if I chose to play;
For the worst is this after all; if they knew me,
  Not a soul upon earth would pity me.

And I play not for pity of these; but you,
  If you saw with your soul what man am I,
You would praise me at least that my soul all through
  Clove to you, loathing the lives that lie;
The souls and lips that are bought and sold,
The smiles of silver and kisses of gold,
The lapdog loves that whine as they chew,
  The little lovers that curse and cry.
There are fairer women, I hear; that may be;
  But I, that I love you and find you fair,
Who are more than fair in my eyes if they be,
  Do the high gods know or the great gods care?
Though the swords in my heart for one were seven,
Would the iron hollow of doubtful heaven,
That knows not itself whether night-time or day be,
  Reverberate words and a foolish prayer?

I will go back to the great sweet mother,
  Mother and lover of men, the sea.
I will go down to her, I and none other,
  Close with her, kiss her and mix her with me;
Cling to her, strive with her, hold her fast:
O fair white mother, in days long past
Born without sister, born without brother,
  Set free my soul as thy soul is free.

O fair green-girdled mother of mine,
  Sea, that art clothed with the sun and the rain,
Thy sweet hard kisses are strong like wine,
  Thy large embraces are keen like pain.
Save me and hide me with all thy waves,
Find me one grave of thy thousand graves,
Those pure cold populous graves of thine
  Wrought without hand in a world without stain.

I shall sleep, and move with the moving ships,
  Change as the winds change, veer in the tide;
My lips will feast on the foam of thy lips,
  I shall rise with thy rising, with thee subside;
Sleep, and not know if she be, if she were,
Filled full with life to the eyes and hair,
As a rose is fulfilled to the roseleaf tips
  With splendid summer and perfume and pride.
This woven raiment of nights and days,
  Were it once cast off and unwound from me,
Naked and glad would I walk in thy ways,
  Alive and aware of thy ways and thee;
Clear of the whole world, hidden at home,
Clothed with the green and crowned with the foam,
A pulse of the life of thy straits and bays,
  A vein in the heart of the streams of the sea.

Fair mother, fed with the lives of men,
  Thou art subtle and cruel of heart, men say.
Thou hast taken, and shalt not render again;
  Thou art full of thy dead, and cold as they.
But death is the worst that comes of thee;
Thou art fed with our dead, O mother, O sea,
But when hast thou fed on our hearts? or when,
  Having given us love, hast thou taken away?

O tender-hearted, O perfect lover,
  Thy lips are bitter, and sweet thine heart.
The hopes that hurt and the dreams that hover,
  Shall they not vanish away and apart?
But thou, thou art sure, thou art older than earth;
Thou art strong for death and fruitful of birth;
Thy depths conceal and thy gulfs discover;
  From the first thou wert; in the end thou art.

And grief shall endure not for ever, I know.
  As things that are not shall these things be;
We shall live through seasons of sun and of snow,
  And none be grievous as this to me.
We shall hear, as one in a trance that hears,
The sound of time, the rhyme of the years;
Wrecked hope and passionate pain will grow
  As tender things of a spring-tide sea.
Sea-fruit that swings in the waves that hiss,
  Drowned gold and purple and royal rings.
And all time past, was it all for this?
  Times unforgotten, and treasures of things?
Swift years of liking and sweet long laughter,
That wist not well of the years thereafter
Till love woke, smitten at heart by a kiss,
  With lips that trembled and trailing wings?

There lived a singer in France of old

By the tideless dolorous midland sea.
In a land of sand and ruin and gold
  There shone one woman, and none but she.
And finding life for her love's sake fail,
Being fain to see her, he bade set sail,
Touched land, and saw her as life grew cold,
  And praised God, seeing; and so died he.

Died, praising God for his gift and grace:
  For she bowed down to him weeping, and said
"Live;" and her tears were shed on his face
  Or ever the life in his face was shed.
The sharp tears fell through her hair, and stung
Once, and her close lips touched him and clung
Once, and grew one with his lips for a space;
  And so drew back, and the man was dead.

O brother, the gods were good to you.
  Sleep, and be glad while the world endures.
Be well content as the years wear through;
  Give thanks for life, and the loves and lures;
Give thanks for life, O brother, and death,
For the sweet last sound of her feet, her breath,
For gifts she gave you, gracious and few,
  Tears and kisses, that lady of yours.
Rest, and be glad of the gods; but I,
  How shall I praise them, or how take rest?
There is not room under all the sky
  For me that know not of worst or best,
Dream or desire of the days before,
Sweet things or bitterness, any more.
Love will not come to me now though I die,
  As love came close to you, breast to breast.

I shall never be friends again with roses;
  I shall loathe sweet tunes, where a note grown strong

Relents and recoils, and climbs and closes,
  As a wave of the sea turned back by song.
There are sounds where the soul's delight takes fire,
Face to face with its own desire;
A delight that rebels, a desire that reposes;
  I shall hate sweet music my whole life long.

The pulse of war and passion of wonder,
  The heavens that murmur, the sounds that shine,
The stars that sing and the loves that thunder,
  The music burning at heart like wine,
An armed archangel whose hands raise up
All senses mixed in the spirit's cup
Till flesh and spirit are molten in sunder--
  These things are over, and no more mine.

These were a part of the playing I heard
  Once, ere my love and my heart were at strife;
Love that sings and hath wings as a bird,
  Balm of the wound and heft of the knife.
Fairer than earth is the sea, and sleep
Than overwatching of eyes that weep,

Now time has done with his one sweet word,
  The wine and leaven of lovely life.

I shall go my ways, tread out my measure,
  Fill the days of my daily breath
With fugitive things not good to treasure,
  Do as the world doth, say as it saith;
But if we had loved each other--O sweet,
Had you felt, lying under the palms of your feet,
The heart of my heart, beating harder with pleasure
  To feel you tread it to dust and death--

Ah, had I not taken my life up and given
  All that life gives and the years let go,
The wine and honey, the balm and leaven,
  The dreams reared high and the hopes brought low?
Come life, come death, not a word be said;
Should I lose you living, and vex you dead?
I never shall tell you on earth; and in heaven,
  If I cry to you then, will you hear or know?

LES NOYADES

Whatever a man of the sons of men
  Shall say to his heart of the lords above,
They have shown man verily, once and again,
  Marvelous mercies and infinite love.

In the wild fifth year of the change of things,
  When France was glorious and blood-red, fair
With dust of battle and deaths of kings,
  A queen of men, with helmeted hair,

Carrier came down to the Loire and slew,
  Till all the ways and the waves waxed red:
Bound and drowned, slaying two by two,
  Maidens and young men, naked and wed.

They brought on a day to his judgment-place
  One rough with labour and red with fight,
And a lady noble by name and face,
  Faultless, a maiden, wonderful, white.

She knew not, being for shame's sake blind,
  If his eyes were hot on her face hard by.
And the judge bade strip and ship them, and bind
  Bosom to bosom, to drown and die.

The white girl winced and whitened; but he
  Caught fire, waxed bright as a great bright flame
Seen with thunder far out on the sea,
  Laughed hard as the glad blood went and came.

Twice his lips quailed with delight, then said,
  "I have but a word to you all, one word;

Bear with me; surely I am but dead;"
  And all they laughed and mocked him and heard.

"Judge, when they open the judgment-roll,
  I will stand upright before God and pray:
'Lord God, have mercy on one man's soul,
  For his mercy was great upon earth, I say.

"'Lord, if I loved thee--Lord, if I served--
  If these who darkened thy fair Son's face
I fought with, sparing not one, nor swerved
  A hand's-breadth, Lord, in the perilous place--

"'I pray thee say to this man, O Lord,
  Sit thou for him at my feet on a throne.
I will face thy wrath, though it bite as a sword,
  And my soul shall burn for his soul, and atone.

"'For, Lord, thou knowest, O God most wise,
  How gracious on earth were his deeds towards me.
Shall this be a small thing in thine eyes,
  That is greater in mine than the whole great sea?'

"I have loved this woman my whole life long,
  And even for love's sake when have I said
'I love you'? when have I done you wrong,
  Living? but now I shall have you dead.

"Yea, now, do I bid you love me, love?
  Love me or loathe, we are one not twain.
But God be praised in his heaven above
  For this my pleasure and that my pain!

"For never a man, being mean like me,
  Shall die like me till the whole world dies.
I shall drown with her, laughing for love; and she

Mix with me, touching me, lips and eyes.

"Shall she not know me and see me all through,
  Me, on whose heart as a worm she trod?
You have given me, God requite it you,
  What man yet never was given of God."

O sweet one love, O my life's delight,
  Dear, though the days have divided us,
Lost beyond hope, taken far out of sight,
  Not twice in the world shall the gods do thus.

Had it been so hard for my love? but I,
  Though the gods gave all that a god can give,
I had chosen rather the gift to die,
  Cease, and be glad above all that live.

For the Loire would have driven us down to the sea,
  And the sea would have pitched us from shoal to shoal;
And I should have held you, and you held me,
  As flesh holds flesh, and the soul the soul.

Could I change you, help you to love me, sweet,
  Could I give you the love that would sweeten death,
We should yield, go down, locked hands and feet,
  Die, drown together, and breath catch breath;

But you would have felt my soul in a kiss,
  And known that once if I loved you well;
And I would have given my soul for this
  To burn for ever in burning hell.

A LEAVE-TAKING

Let us go hence, my songs; she will not hear.
Let us go hence together without fear;
Keep silence now, for singing-time is over,
And over all old things and all things dear.
She loves not you nor me as all we love her.
Yea, though we sang as angels in her ear,
    She would not hear.

Let us rise up and part; she will not know.
Let us go seaward as the great winds go,
Full of blown sand and foam; what help is here?
There is no help, for all these things are so,
And all the world is bitter as a tear.
And how these things are, though ye strove to show,
    She would not know.

Let us go home and hence; she will not weep.
We gave love many dreams and days to keep,
Flowers without scent, and fruits that would not grow,
Saying 'If thou wilt, thrust in thy sickle and reap.'
All is reaped now; no grass is left to mow;
And we that sowed, though all we fell on sleep,
    She would not weep.

Let us go hence and rest; she will not love.
She shall not hear us if we sing hereof,
Nor see love's ways, how sore they are and steep.
Come hence, let be, lie still; it is enough.
Love is a barren sea, bitter and deep;
And though she saw all heaven in flower above,
    She would not love.

Let us give up, go down; she will not care.
Though all the stars made gold of all the air,
And the sea moving saw before it move

One moon-flower making all the foam-flowers fair;
Though all those waves went over us, and drove
Deep down the stifling lips and drowning hair,
   She would not care.

Let us go hence, go hence; she will not see.
Sing all once more together; surely she,
She too, remembering days and words that were,
Will turn a little toward us, sighing; but we,
We are hence, we are gone, as though we had not been there.
  Nay, and though all men seeing had pity on me,
   She would not see.

ITYLUS

Swallow, my sister, O sister swallow,
  How can thine heart be full of the spring?
    A thousand summers are over and dead.
What hast thou found in the spring to follow?
  What hast thou found in thine heart to sing?
    What wilt thou do when the summer is shed?

O swallow, sister, O fair swift swallow,
  Why wilt thou fly after spring to the south,
    The soft south whither thine heart is set?
Shall not the grief of the old time follow?
  Shall not the song thereof cleave to thy mouth?
    Hast thou forgotten ere I forget?

Sister, my sister, O fleet sweet swallow,
  Thy way is long to the sun and the south;
    But I, fulfilled of my heart's desire,
Shedding my song upon height, upon hollow,
  From tawny body and sweet small mouth
    Feed the heart of the night with fire.

I the nightingale all spring through,
  O swallow, sister, O changing swallow,
    All spring through till the spring be done,
Clothed with the light of the night on the dew,
  Sing, while the hours and the wild birds follow,
    Take flight and follow and find the sun.

Sister, my sister, O soft light swallow,
  Though all things feast in the spring's guest-chamber,
    How hast thou heart to be glad thereof yet?
For where thou fliest I shall not follow,
  Till life forget and death remember,
    Till thou remember and I forget.

Swallow, my sister, O singing swallow,
　I know not how thou hast heart to sing.
　　Hast thou the heart? is it all past over?
Thy lord the summer is good to follow,
　And fair the feet of thy lover the spring:
　　But what wilt thou say to the spring thy lover?

O swallow, sister, O fleeting swallow,
　My heart in me is a molten ember
　　And over my head the waves have met.
But thou wouldst tarry or I would follow,
　Could I forget or thou remember,
　　Couldst thou remember and I forget.

O sweet stray sister, O shifting swallow,
　The heart's division divideth us.
　　Thy heart is light as a leaf of a tree;
But mine goes forth among sea-gulfs hollow
　To the place of the slaying of Itylus,
　　The feast of Daulis, the Thracian sea.

O swallow, sister, O rapid swallow,
　I pray thee sing not a little space.
　　Are not the roofs and the lintels wet?
The woven web that was plain to follow,
　The small slain body, the flowerlike face,
　　Can I remember if thou forget?

O sister, sister, thy first-begotten!
　The hands that cling and the feet that follow,
　　The voice of the child's blood crying yet
Who hath remembered me? who hath forgotten?
　Thou hast forgotten, O summer swallow,
　　But the world shall end when I forget.

ANACTORIA

[Greek: tinos au ty peithoi maps sagêneusas philotata?]
SAPPHO.

1 My life is bitter with thy love; thine eyes
2 Blind me, thy tresses burn me, thy sharp sighs
3 Divide my flesh and spirit with soft sound,
4 And my blood strengthens, and my veins abound.
5 I pray thee sigh not, speak not, draw not breath;
6 Let life burn down, and dream it is not death.
7 I would the sea had hidden us, the fire
8 (Wilt thou fear that, and fear not my desire?)
9 Severed the bones that bleach, the flesh that cleaves,
10 And let our sifted ashes drop like leaves.
11 I feel thy blood against my blood: my pain
12 Pains thee, and lips bruise lips, and vein stings vein.
13 Let fruit be crushed on fruit, let flower on flower,
14 Breast kindle breast, and either burn one hour.
15 Why wilt thou follow lesser loves? are thine
16 Too weak to bear these hands and lips of mine?
17 I charge thee for my life's sake, O too sweet
18 To crush love with thy cruel faultless feet,
19 I charge thee keep thy lips from hers or his,
20 Sweetest, till theirs be sweeter than my kiss.
21 Lest I too lure, a swallow for a dove,
22 Erotion or Erinna to my love.
23 I would my love could kill thee; I am satiated
24 With seeing thee live, and fain would have thee dead.
25 I would earth had thy body as fruit to eat,
26 And no mouth but some serpent's found thee sweet.
27 I would find grievous ways to have thee slain,
28 Intense device, and superflux of pain;
29 Vex thee with amorous agonies, and shake
30 Life at thy lips, and leave it there to ache;
31 Strain out thy soul with pangs too soft to kill,

32 Intolerable interludes, and infinite ill;
33 Relapse and reluctation of the breath,
34 Dumb tunes and shuddering semitones of death.
35 I am weary of all thy words and soft strange ways,
36 Of all love's fiery nights and all his days,
37 And all the broken kisses salt as brine
38 That shuddering lips make moist with waterish wine,
39 And eyes the bluer for all those hidden hours
40 That pleasure fills with tears and feeds from flowers,
41 Fierce at the heart with fire that half comes through,
42 But all the flowerlike white stained round with blue;
43 The fervent underlid, and that above
44 Lifted with laughter or abashed with love;
45 Thine amorous girdle, full of thee and fair,
46 And leavings of the lilies in thine hair.
47 Yea, all sweet words of thine and all thy ways,
48 And all the fruit of nights and flower of days,
49 And stinging lips wherein the hot sweet brine
50 That Love was born of burns and foams like wine,
51 And eyes insatiable of amorous hours,
52 Fervent as fire and delicate as flowers,
53 Coloured like night at heart, but cloven through
54 Like night with flame, dyed round like night with blue,
55 Clothed with deep eyelids under and above--
56 Yea, all thy beauty sickens me with love;
57 Thy girdle empty of thee and now not fair,
58 And ruinous lilies in thy languid hair.
59 Ah, take no thought for Love's sake; shall this be,
60 And she who loves thy lover not love thee?
61 Sweet soul, sweet mouth of all that laughs and lives,
62 Mine is she, very mine; and she forgives.
63 For I beheld in sleep the light that is
64 In her high place in Paphos, heard the kiss
65 Of body and soul that mix with eager tears
66 And laughter stinging through the eyes and ears;
67 Saw Love, as burning flame from crown to feet,

68 Imperishable, upon her storied seat;
69 Clear eyelids lifted toward the north and south,
70 A mind of many colours, and a mouth
71 Of many tunes and kisses; and she bowed,
72 With all her subtle face laughing aloud,
73 Bowed down upon me, saying, "Who doth thee wrong,
74 Sappho?" but thou--thy body is the song,
75 Thy mouth the music; thou art more than I,
76 Though my voice die not till the whole world die;
77 Though men that hear it madden; though love weep,
78 Though nature change, though shame be charmed to sleep.
79 Ah, wilt thou slay me lest I kiss thee dead?
80 Yet the queen laughed from her sweet heart and said:
81 "Even she that flies shall follow for thy sake,
82 And she shall give thee gifts that would not take,
83 Shall kiss that would not kiss thee" (yea, kiss me)
84 "When thou wouldst not"--when I would not kiss thee!
85 Ah, more to me than all men as thou art,
86 Shall not my songs assuage her at the heart?
87 Ah, sweet to me as life seems sweet to death,
88 Why should her wrath fill thee with fearful breath?
89 Nay, sweet, for is she God alone? hath she
90 Made earth and all the centuries of the sea,
91 Taught the sun ways to travel, woven most fine
92 The moonbeams, shed the starbeams forth as wine,
93 Bound with her myrtles, beaten with her rods,
94 The young men and the maidens and the gods?
95 Have we not lips to love with, eyes for tears,
96 And summer and flower of women and of years?
97 Stars for the foot of morning, and for noon
98 Sunlight, and exaltation of the moon;
99 Waters that answer waters, fields that wear
100 Lilies, and languor of the Lesbian air?
101 Beyond those flying feet of fluttered doves,
102 Are there not other gods for other loves?
103 Yea, though she scourge thee, sweetest, for my sake,

Blossom not thorns and flowers not blood should break.
Ah that my lips were tuneless lips, but pressed
To the bruised blossom of thy scourged white breast!
Ah that my mouth for Muses' milk were fed
On the sweet blood thy sweet small wounds had bled!
That with my tongue I felt them, and could taste
The faint flakes from thy bosom to the waist!
That I could drink thy veins as wine, and eat
Thy breasts like honey! that from face to feet
Thy body were abolished and consumed,
And in my flesh thy very flesh entombed!
Ah, ah, thy beauty! like a beast it bites,
Stings like an adder, like an arrow smites.
Ah sweet, and sweet again, and seven times sweet,
The paces and the pauses of thy feet!
Ah sweeter than all sleep or summer air
The fallen fillets fragrant from thine hair!
Yea, though their alien kisses do me wrong,
Sweeter thy lips than mine with all their song;
Thy shoulders whiter than a fleece of white,
And flower-sweet fingers, good to bruise or bite
As honeycomb of the inmost honey-cells,
With almond-shaped and roseleaf-coloured shells
And blood like purple blossom at the tips
Quivering; and pain made perfect in thy lips
For my sake when I hurt thee; O that I
Durst crush thee out of life with love, and die,
Die of thy pain and my delight, and be
Mixed with thy blood and molten into thee!
Would I not plague thee dying overmuch?
Would I not hurt thee perfectly? not touch
Thy pores of sense with torture, and make bright
Thine eyes with bloodlike tears and grievous light?
Strike pang from pang as note is struck from note,
Catch the sob's middle music in thy throat,
Take thy limbs living, and new-mould with these

A lyre of many faultless agonies?
Feed thee with fever and famine and fine drouth,
With perfect pangs convulse thy perfect mouth,
Make thy life shudder in thee and burn afresh,
And wring thy very spirit through the flesh?
Cruel? but love makes all that love him well
As wise as heaven and crueller than hell.
Me hath love made more bitter toward thee
Than death toward man; but were I made as he
Who hath made all things to break them one by one,
If my feet trod upon the stars and sun
And souls of men as his have alway trod,
God knows I might be crueller than God.
For who shall change with prayers or thanksgivings
The mystery of the cruelty of things?
Or say what God above all gods and years
With offering and blood-sacrifice of tears,
With lamentation from strange lands, from graves
Where the snake pastures, from scarred mouths of slaves,
From prison, and from plunging prows of ships
Through flamelike foam of the sea's closing lips--
With thwartings of strange signs, and wind-blown hair
Of comets, desolating the dim air,
When darkness is made fast with seals and bars,
And fierce reluctance of disastrous stars,
Eclipse, and sound of shaken hills, and wings
Darkening, and blind inexpiable things--
With sorrow of labouring moons, and altering light
And travail of the planets of the night,
And weeping of the weary Pleiads seven,
Feeds the mute melancholy lust of heaven?
Is not his incense bitterness, his meat
Murder? his hidden face and iron feet
Hath not man known, and felt them on their way
Threaten and trample all things and every day?
Hath he not sent us hunger? who hath cursed

Spirit and flesh with longing? filled with thirst
Their lips who cried unto him? who bade exceed
The fervid will, fall short the feeble deed,
Bade sink the spirit and the flesh aspire,
Pain animate the dust of dead desire,
And life yield up her flower to violent fate?
Him would I reach, him smite, him desecrate,
Pierce the cold lips of God with human breath,
And mix his immortality with death.
Why hath he made us? what had all we done
That we should live and loathe the sterile sun,
And with the moon wax paler as she wanes,
And pulse by pulse feel time grow through our veins?
Thee too the years shall cover; thou shalt be
As the rose born of one same blood with thee,
As a song sung, as a word said, and fall
Flower-wise, and be not any more at all,
Nor any memory of thee anywhere;
For never Muse has bound above thine hair
The high Pierian flower whose graft outgrows
All summer kinship of the mortal rose
And colour of deciduous days, nor shed
Reflex and flush of heaven about thine head,
Nor reddened brows made pale by floral grief
With splendid shadow from that lordlier leaf.
Yea, thou shalt be forgotten like spilt wine,
Except these kisses of my lips on thine
Brand them with immortality; but me--
Men shall not see bright fire nor hear the sea,
Nor mix their hearts with music, nor behold
Cast forth of heaven, with feet of awful gold
And plumeless wings that make the bright air blind,
Lightning, with thunder for a hound behind
Hunting through fields unfurrowed and unsown,
But in the light and laughter, in the moan
And music, and in grasp of lip and hand

90

11 And shudder of water that makes felt on land
12 The immeasurable tremor of all the sea,
13 Memories shall mix and metaphors of me.
14 Like me shall be the shuddering calm of night,
15 When all the winds of the world for pure delight
16 Close lips that quiver and fold up wings that ache;
17 When nightingales are louder for love's sake,
18 And leaves tremble like lute-strings or like fire;
19 Like me the one star swooning with desire
20 Even at the cold lips of the sleepless moon,
21 As I at thine; like me the waste white noon,
22 Burnt through with barren sunlight; and like me
23 The land-stream and the tide-stream in the sea.
24 I am sick with time as these with ebb and flow,
25 And by the yearning in my veins I know
26 The yearning sound of waters; and mine eyes
27 Burn as that beamless fire which fills the skies
28 With troubled stars and travailing things of flame;
29 And in my heart the grief consuming them
30 Labours, and in my veins the thirst of these,
31 And all the summer travail of the trees
32 And all the winter sickness; and the earth,
33 Filled full with deadly works of death and birth,
34 Sore spent with hungry lusts of birth and death,
35 Has pain like mine in her divided breath;
36 Her spring of leaves is barren, and her fruit
37 Ashes; her boughs are burdened, and her root
38 Fibrous and gnarled with poison; underneath
39 Serpents have gnawn it through with tortuous teeth
40 Made sharp upon the bones of all the dead,
41 And wild birds rend her branches overhead.
42 These, woven as raiment for his word and thought,
43 These hath God made, and me as these, and wrought
44 Song, and hath lit it at my lips; and me
45 Earth shall not gather though she feed on thee.
46 As a shed tear shalt thou be shed; but I--

247 Lo, earth may labour, men live long and die,
248 Years change and stars, and the high God devise
249 New things, and old things wane before his eyes
250 Who wields and wrecks them, being more strong than
251 they--
252 But, having made me, me he shall not slay.
253 Nor slay nor satiate, like those herds of his
254 Who laugh and live a little, and their kiss
255 Contents them, and their loves are swift and sweet,
256 And sure death grasps and gains them with slow feet,
257 Love they or hate they, strive or bow their knees--
258 And all these end; he hath his will of these.
259 Yea, but albeit he slay me, hating me--
260 Albeit he hide me in the deep dear sea
261 And cover me with cool wan foam, and ease
262 This soul of mine as any soul of these,
263 And give me water and great sweet waves, and make
264 The very sea's name lordlier for my sake,
265 The whole sea sweeter--albeit I die indeed
266 And hide myself and sleep and no man heed,
267 Of me the high God hath not all his will.
268 Blossom of branches, and on each high hill
269 Clear air and wind, and under in clamorous vales
270 Fierce noises of the fiery nightingales,
271 Buds burning in the sudden spring like fire,
272 The wan washed sand and the waves' vain desire,
273 Sails seen like blown white flowers at sea, and words
274 That bring tears swiftest, and long notes of birds
275 Violently singing till the whole world sings--
276 I Sappho shall be one with all these things,
277 With all high things for ever; and my face
278 Seen once, my songs once heard in a strange place,
279 Cleave to men's lives, and waste the days thereof
280 With gladness and much sadness and long love.
281 Yea, they shall say, earth's womb has borne in vain
282 New things, and never this best thing again;

Borne days and men, borne fruits and wars and wine,
Seasons and songs, but no song more like mine.
And they shall know me as ye who have known me here,
Last year when I loved Atthis, and this year
When I love thee; and they shall praise me, and say
"She hath all time as all we have our day,
Shall she not live and have her will"--even I?
Yea, though thou diest, I say I shall not die.
For these shall give me of their souls, shall give
Life, and the days and loves wherewith I live,
Shall quicken me with loving, fill with breath,
Save me and serve me, strive for me with death.
Alas, that neither moon nor snow nor dew
Nor all cold things can purge me wholly through,
Assuage me nor allay me nor appease,
Till supreme sleep shall bring me bloodless ease;
Till time wax faint in all his periods;
Till fate undo the bondage of the gods,
And lay, to slake and satiate me all through,
Lotus and Lethe on my lips like dew,
And shed around and over and under me
Thick darkness and the insuperable sea.

HYMN TO PROSERPINE

(AFTER THE PROCLAMATION IN ROME OF THE CHRISTIAN FAITH)

Vicisti, Galilæe.

I have lived long enough, having seen one thing, that love hath an end;
Goddess and maiden and queen, be near me now and befriend.
Thou art more than the day or the morrow, the seasons that laugh or that weep;
For these give joy and sorrow; but thou, Proserpina, sleep.
Sweet is the treading of wine, and sweet the feet of the dove;
But a goodlier gift is thine than foam of the grapes or love.
Yea, is not even Apollo, with hair and harpstring of gold,
A bitter God to follow, a beautiful God to behold?
I am sick of singing: the bays burn deep and chafe: I am fain
To rest a little from praise and grievous pleasure and pain.
For the Gods we know not of, who give us our daily breath,
We know they are cruel as love or life, and lovely as death.
O Gods dethroned and deceased, cast forth, wiped out in a day!
From your wrath is the world released, redeemed from your chains, men say.
New Gods are crowned in the city; their flowers have broken your rods;
They are merciful, clothed with pity, the young compassionate Gods.

But for me their new device is barren, the days are bare;
Things long past over suffice, and men forgotten that were.
Time and the Gods are at strife; ye dwell in the midst thereof,
Draining a little life from the barren breasts of love.
I say to you, cease, take rest; yea, I say to you all, be at peace,
Till the bitter milk of her breast and the barren bosom shall cease.
Wilt thou yet take all, Galilean? but these thou shalt not take,
The laurel, the palms and the pæan, the breasts of the nymphs in the brake;
Breasts more soft than a dove's, that tremble with tenderer breath;
And all the wings of the Loves, and all the joy before death;
All the feet of the hours that sound as a single lyre,
Dropped and deep in the flowers, with strings that flicker like fire.
More than these wilt thou give, things fairer than all these things?
Nay, for a little we live, and life hath mutable wings.
A little while and we die; shall life not thrive as it may?
For no man under the sky lives twice, outliving his day.
And grief is a grievous thing, and a man hath enough of his tears:
Why should he labour, and bring fresh grief to blacken his years?
Thou hast conquered, O pale Galilean; the world has grown grey from thy breath;
We have drunken of things Lethean, and fed on the fullness of death.
Laurel is green for a season, and love is sweet for a day;

But love grows bitter with treason, and laurel outlives not May.

Sleep, shall we sleep after all? for the world is not sweet in the end;

For the old faiths loosen and fall, the new years ruin and rend.

Fate is a sea without shore, and the soul is a rock that abides;

But her ears are vexed with the roar and her face with the foam of the tides.

O lips that the live blood faints in, the leavings of racks and rods!

O ghastly glories of saints, dead limbs of gibbeted Gods!

Though all men abase them before you in spirit, and all knees bend,

I kneel not neither adore you, but standing, look to the end.

All delicate days and pleasant, all spirits and sorrows are cast

Far out with the foam of the present that sweeps to the surf of the past:

Where beyond the extreme sea-wall, and between the remote sea-gates,

Waste water washes, and tall ships founder, and deep death waits:

Where, mighty with deepening sides, clad about with the seas as with wings,

And impelled of invisible tides, and fulfilled of unspeakable things,

White-eyed and poisonous-finned, shark-toothed and serpentine-curled,

Rolls, under the whitening wind of the future, the wave of the world.

The depths stand naked in sunder behind it, the storms flee away;

In the hollow before it the thunder is taken and snared as a prey;

In its sides is the north-wind bound; and its salt is of all men's tears;

With light of ruin, and sound of changes, and pulse of years:

With travail of day after day, and with trouble of hour upon hour;

And bitter as blood is the spray; and the crests are as fangs that devour:

And its vapour and storm of its steam as the sighing of spirits to be;

And its noise as the noise in a dream; and its depth as the roots of he sea:

And the height of its heads as the height of the utmost stars of the air:

And the ends of the earth at the might thereof tremble, and time is made bare.

Will ye bridle the deep sea with reins, will ye chasten the high sea with rods?

Will ye take her to chain her with chains, who is older than all ye Gods?

All ye as a wind shall go by, as a fire shall ye pass and be past;

Ye are Gods, and behold, ye shall die, and the waves be upon you at last.

In the darkness of time, in the deeps of the years, in the changes of things,

Ye shall sleep as a slain man sleeps, and the world shall forget you for kings.

Though the feet of thine high priests tread where thy lords and our forefathers trod,

Though these that were Gods are dead, and thou being dead art a God,

Though before thee the throned Cytherean be fallen, and hidden her head,

Yet thy kingdom shall pass, Galilean, thy dead shall go down to thee dead.

Of the maiden thy mother men sing as a goddess with grace clad around;

Thou art throned where another was king; where another was queen she is crowned.

Yea, once we had sight of another: but now she is queen, say these.

Not as thine, not as thine was our mother, a blossom of flowering seas,

Clothed round with the world's desire as with raiment, and fair as the foam,

And fleeter than kindled fire, and a goddess, and mother of Rome.

For thine came pale and a maiden, and sister to sorrow; but ours,

Her deep hair heavily laden with odour and colour of flowers,

White rose of the rose-white water, a silver splendour, a flame,

Bent down unto us that besought her, and earth grew sweet with her name.

For thine came weeping, a slave among slaves, and rejected; but she

Came flushed from the full-flushed wave, and imperial, her foot on the sea.

And the wonderful waters knew her, the winds and the viewless ways,

And the roses grew rosier, and bluer the sea-blue stream of the bays.

Ye are fallen, our lords, by what token? we wist that ye should not fall.

Ye were all so fair that are broken; and one more fair than ye all.

But I turn to her still, having seen she shall surely abide in the end;

Goddess and maiden and queen, be near me now and befriend.

O daughter of earth, of my mother, her crown and blossom of birth,

I am also, I also, thy brother; I go as I came unto earth.

In the night where thine eyes are as moons are in heaven, the night where thou art,

Where the silence is more than all tunes, where sleep overflows from the heart,

Where the poppies are sweet as the rose in our world, and the red rose is white,

And the wind falls faint as it blows with the fume of the flowers of the night,

And the murmur of spirits that sleep in the shadow of Gods from afar

Grows dim in thine ears and deep as the deep dim soul of a star,

In the sweet low light of thy face, under heavens untrod by the sun,

Let my soul with their souls find place, and forget what is done and undone.

Thou art more than the Gods who number the days of our temporal breath:

For these give labour and slumber; but thou, Proserpina, death.

Therefore now at thy feet I abide for a season in silence. I know

I shall die as my fathers died, and sleep as they sleep; even so.

For the glass of the years is brittle wherein we gaze for a span;

A little soul for a little bears up this corpse which is man. [2]

So long I endure, no longer; and laugh not again, neither weep.

For there is no God found stronger than death; and death is a sleep.

[2] [Greek: psycharion ei bastazon nekron].

EPICTETUS

ILICET
 There is an end of joy and sorrow;
 Peace all day long, all night, all morrow,
  But never a time to laugh or weep.
 The end is come of pleasant places,
 The end of tender words and faces,
  The end of all, the poppied sleep.

No place for sound within their hearing,
No room to hope, no time for fearing,
 No lips to laugh, no lids for tears.
The old years have run out all their measure;
No chance of pain, no chance of pleasure,
 No fragment of the broken years.
Outside of all the worlds and ages,
There where the fool is as the sage is,
 There where the slayer is clean of blood,
No end, no passage, no beginning,
There where the sinner leaves off sinning,
 There where the good man is not good.

There is not one thing with another,
But Evil saith to Good: My brother,
 My brother, I am one with thee:
They shall not strive nor cry for ever:
No man shall choose between them: never
 Shall this thing end and that thing be.

Wind wherein seas and stars are shaken
Shall shake them, and they shall not waken;
 None that has lain down shall arise;
The stones are sealed across their places;
One shadow is shed on all their faces,
 One blindness cast on all their eyes.

Sleep, is it sleep perchance that covers
Each face, as each face were his lover's?
  Farewell; as men that sleep fare well.
The grave's mouth laughs unto derision
Desire and dread and dream and vision,
  Delight of heaven and sorrow of hell.

No soul shall tell nor lip shall number
The names and tribes of you that slumber;
  No memory, no memorial.
"Thou knowest"--who shall say thou knowest?
There is none highest and none lowest:
  An end, an end, an end of all.

Good night, good sleep, good rest from sorrow
To these that shall not have good morrow;
  The gods be gentle to all these.
Nay, if death be not, how shall they be?
Nay, is there help in heaven? it may be
  All things and lords of things shall cease.

The stooped urn, filling, dips and flashes;
The bronzèd brims are deep in ashes;
  The pale old lips of death are fed.
Shall this dust gather flesh hereafter?
Shall one shed tears or fall to laughter,
  At sight of all these poor old dead?

Nay, as thou wilt; these know not of it;
Thine eyes' strong weeping shall not profit,
  Thy laughter shall not give thee ease;
Cry aloud, spare not, cease not crying,
Sigh, till thou cleave thy sides with sighing,
  Thou shalt not raise up one of these.

Burnt spices flash, and burnt wine hisses,
The breathing flame's mouth curls and kisses
  The small dried rows of frankincense;
All round the sad red blossoms smoulder,
Flowers coloured like the fire, but colder,
  In sign of sweet things taken hence;

Yea, for their sake and in death's favour
Things of sweet shape and of sweet savour
  We yield them, spice and flower and wine;
Yea, costlier things than wine or spices,
Whereof none knoweth how great the price is,
  And fruit that comes not of the vine.

From boy's pierced throat and girl's pierced bosom
Drips, reddening round the blood-red blossom,
  The slow delicious bright soft blood,
Bathing the spices and the pyre,
Bathing the flowers and fallen fire,
  Bathing the blossom by the bud.

Roses whose lips the flame has deadened
Drink till the lapping leaves are reddened
  And warm wet inner petals weep;
The flower whereof sick sleep gets leisure,
Barren of balm and purple pleasure,
  Fumes with no native steam of sleep.

Why will ye weep? what do ye weeping?
For waking folk and people sleeping,
  And sands that fill and sands that fall,
The days rose-red, the poppied hours,

Blood, wine, and spice and fire and flowers,
  There is one end of one and all.

Shall such an one lend love or borrow?
Shall these be sorry for thy sorrow?
  Shall these give thanks for words or breath?
Their hate is as their loving-kindness;
The frontlet of their brows is blindness,
  The armlet of their arms is death.

Lo, for no noise or light of thunder
Shall these grave-clothes be rent in sunder;
  He that hath taken, shall he give?
He hath rent them: shall he bind together?
He hath bound them: shall he break the tether?
  He hath slain them: shall he bid them live?

A little sorrow, a little pleasure,
Fate metes us from the dusty measure
  That holds the date of all of us;
We are born with travail and strong crying,
And from the birth-day to the dying
  The likeness of our life is thus.

One girds himself to serve another,
Whose father was the dust, whose mother
  The little dead red worm therein;
They find no fruit of things they cherish;
The goodness of a man shall perish,
  It shall be one thing with his sin.

In deep wet ways by grey old gardens
Fed with sharp spring the sweet fruit hardens;
  They know not what fruits wane or grow;
Red summer burns to the utmost ember;
They know not, neither can remember,
  The old years and flowers they used to know.

Ah, for their sakes, so trapped and taken,

For theirs, forgotten and forsaken,
  Watch, sleep not, gird thyself with prayer.
Nay, where the heart of wrath is broken,
Where long love ends as a thing spoken,
  How shall thy crying enter there?

Though the iron sides of the old world falter,
The likeness of them shall not alter
  For all the rumour of periods,
The stars and seasons that come after,
The tears of latter men, the laughter
  Of the old unalterable gods.

Far up above the years and nations,
The high gods, clothed and crowned with patience,
  Endure through days of deathlike date;
They bear the witness of things hidden;
Before their eyes all life stands chidden,
  As they before the eyes of Fate.

Not for their love shall Fate retire,
Nor they relent for our desire,
  Nor the graves open for their call.
The end is more than joy and anguish,
Than lives that laugh and lives that languish,
  The poppied sleep, the end of all.

HERMAPHRODITUS

I

Lift up thy lips, turn round, look back for love,
  Blind love that comes by night and casts out rest;
  Of all things tired thy lips look weariest,
Save the long smile that they are wearied of.
Ah sweet, albeit no love be sweet enough,
  Choose of two loves and cleave unto the best;
  Two loves at either blossom of thy breast
Strive until one be under and one above.
Their breath is fire upon the amorous air,
  Fire in thine eyes and where thy lips suspire:
And whosoever hath seen thee, being so fair,
  Two things turn all his life and blood to fire;
A strong desire begot on great despair,
  A great despair cast out by strong desire.

II

Where between sleep and life some brief space is,
  With love like gold bound round about the head,
  Sex to sweet sex with lips and limbs is wed,
Turning the fruitful feud of hers and his
To the waste wedlock of a sterile kiss;
  Yet from them something like as fire is shed
  That shall not be assuaged till death be dead,
Though neither life nor sleep can find out this.
Love made himself of flesh that perisheth
  A pleasure-house for all the loves his kin;
But on the one side sat a man like death,
  And on the other a woman sat like sin.
So with veiled eyes and sobs between his breath
  Love turned himself and would not enter in.

III

Love, is it love or sleep or shadow or light
  That lies between thine eyelids and thine eyes?
  Like a flower laid upon a flower it lies,
Or like the night's dew laid upon the night.
Love stands upon thy left hand and thy right,
Yet by no sunset and by no moonrise
  Shall make thee man and ease a woman's sighs,
  Or make thee woman for a man's delight.
To what strange end hath some strange god made fair
  The double blossom of two fruitless flowers?
Hid love in all the folds of all thy hair,
  Fed thee on summers, watered thee with showers,
Given all the gold that all the seasons wear
  To thee that art a thing of barren hours?

IV

Yea, love, I see; it is not love but fear.
  Nay, sweet, it is not fear but love, I know;
  Or wherefore should thy body's blossom blow
So sweetly, or thine eyelids leave so clear
Thy gracious eyes that never made a tear--
  Though for their love our tears like blood should flow,
  Though love and life and death should come and go,
So dreadful, so desirable, so dear?
Yea, sweet, I know; I saw in what swift wise
  Beneath the woman's and the water's kiss
  Thy moist limbs melted into Salmacis,
And the large light turned tender in thine eyes,

And all thy boy's breath softened into sighs;
  But Love being blind, how should he know of this?

FRAGOLETTA

O Love! what shall be said of thee?
The son of grief begot by joy?
Being sightless, wilt thou see?
Being sexless, wilt thou be
Maiden or boy?

I dreamed of strange lips yesterday
And cheeks wherein the ambiguous blood
Was like a rose's--yea,
A rose's when it lay
Within the bud.

What fields have bred thee, or what groves
Concealed thee, O mysterious flower,
O double rose of Love's,
With leaves that lure the doves
From bud to bower?

I dare not kiss it, lest my lip
Press harder than an indrawn breath,
And all the sweet life slip
Forth, and the sweet leaves drip,
Bloodlike, in death.

O sole desire of my delight!
O sole delight of my desire!
Mine eyelids and eyesight
Feed on thee day and night
Like lips of fire.

Lean back thy throat of carven pearl,
Let thy mouth murmur like the dove's;
Say, Venus hath no girl,
No front of female curl,

Among her Loves.

Thy sweet low bosom, thy close hair,
Thy strait soft flanks and slenderer feet,
Thy virginal strange air,
Are these not over fair
For Love to greet?

How should he greet thee? what new name,
Fit to move all men's hearts, could move
Thee, deaf to love or shame,
Love's sister, by the same
Mother as Love?

Ah sweet, the maiden's mouth is cold,
Her breast-blossoms are simply red,
Her hair mere brown or gold,
Fold over simple fold
Binding her head.

Thy mouth is made of fire and wine,
Thy barren bosom takes my kiss
And turns my soul to thine
And turns thy lip to mine,
And mine it is.

Thou hast a serpent in thine hair,
In all the curls that close and cling;
And ah, thy breast-flower!
Ah love, thy mouth too fair
To kiss and sting!

Cleave to me, love me, kiss mine eyes,
Satiate thy lips with loving me;
Nay, for thou shalt not rise;

Lie still as Love that dies
For love of thee.

Mine arms are close about thine head,
My lips are fervent on thy face,
And where my kiss hath fed
Thy flower-like blood leaps red
To the kissed place.

O bitterness of things too sweet!
O broken singing of the dove!
Love's wings are over fleet,
And like the panther's feet
The feet of Love.

RONDEL

These many years since we began to be,
What have the gods done with us? what with me,
What with my love? they have shown me fates and fears,
Harsh springs, and fountains bitterer than the sea,
Grief a fixed star, and joy a vane that veers,
  These many years.

With her, my love, with her have they done well?
But who shall answer for her? who shall tell
Sweet things or sad, such things as no man hears?
May no tears fall, if no tears ever fell,
From eyes more dear to me than starriest spheres
  These many years!

But if tears ever touched, for any grief,
Those eyelids folded like a white-rose leaf,
Deep double shells wherethrough the eye-flower peers,
Let them weep once more only, sweet and brief,
Brief tears and bright, for one who gave her tears
  These many years.

SATIA TE SANGUINE

If you loved me ever so little,
  I could bear the bonds that gall,
I could dream the bonds were brittle;
  You do not love me at all.

O beautiful lips, O bosom
  More white than the moon's and warm,
A sterile, a ruinous blossom
  Is blown your way in a storm.

As the lost white feverish limbs
  Of the Lesbian Sappho, adrift
In foam where the sea-weed swims,
  Swam loose for the streams to lift,

My heart swims blind in a sea
  That stuns me; swims to and fro,
And gathers to windward and lee
  Lamentation, and mourning, and woe.

A broken, an emptied boat,
  Sea saps it, winds blow apart,
Sick and adrift and afloat,
  The barren waif of a heart.

Where, when the gods would be cruel,
  Do they go for a torture? where
Plant thorns, set pain like a jewel?
  Ah, not in the flesh, not there!

The racks of earth and the rods
  Are weak as foam on the sands;
In the heart is the prey for gods,
  Who crucify hearts, not hands.

Mere pangs corrode and consume,
  Dead when life dies in the brain;
In the infinite spirit is room
  For the pulse of an infinite pain.

I wish you were dead, my dear;
  I would give you, had I to give
Some death too bitter to fear;
  It is better to die than live.

I wish you were stricken of thunder
  And burnt with a bright flame through,
Consumed and cloven in sunder,
  I dead at your feet like you.

If I could but know after all,
  I might cease to hunger and ache,
Though your heart were ever so small,
  If it were not a stone or a snake.

You are crueller, you that we love,
  Than hatred, hunger, or death;
You have eyes and breasts like a dove,
  And you kill men's hearts with a breath

As plague in a poisonous city
  Insults and exults on her dead,
So you, when pallid for pity
  Comes love, and fawns to be fed.

As a tame beast writhes and wheedles,
  He fawns to be fed with wiles;
You carve him a cross of needles,
  And whet them sharp as your smiles.

He is patient of thorn and whip,
  He is dumb under axe or dart;
You suck with a sleepy red lip
  The wet red wounds in his heart.

You thrill as his pulses dwindle,
  You brighten and warm as he bleeds,
With insatiable eyes that kindle
  And insatiable mouth that feeds.

Your hands nailed love to the tree,
  You stript him, scourged him with rods,
And drowned him deep in the sea
  That hides the dead and their gods.

And for all this, die will he not;
  There is no man sees him but I;
You came and went and forgot;
  I hope he will some day die.

A LITANY

[Greek: en ouranô phaennas
krypsô par' hymin augas,
mias pro nyktos hepta nyktas hexete, k.t.l.]
                    Anth. Sac.

FIRST ANTIPHONE

All the bright lights of heaven
    I will make dark over thee;
One night shall be as seven
    That its skirts may cover thee;
I will send on thy strong men a sword,
    On thy remnant a rod;
Ye shall know that I am the Lord,
    Saith the Lord God.

SECOND ANTIPHONE

All the bright lights of heaven
    Thou hast made dark over us;
One night has been as seven
    That its skirt might cover us;
Thou hast sent on our strong men a sword,
    On our remnant a rod;
We know that thou art the Lord,
    O Lord our God.

THIRD ANTIPHONE

As the tresses and wings of the wind
    Are scattered and shaken,

I will scatter all them that have sinned,
    There shall none be taken;
As a sower that scattereth seed,
    So will I scatter them;
As one breaketh and shattereth a reed,
    I will break and shatter them.

FOURTH ANTIPHONE

As the wings and the locks of the wind
    Are scattered and shaken,
Thou hast scattered all them that have sinned,
    There was no man taken;
As a sower that scattereth seed,
    So hast thou scattered us;
As one breaketh and shattereth a reed,
    Thou hast broken and shattered us.

FIFTH ANTIPHONE

From all thy lovers that love thee
    I God will sunder thee;
I will make darkness above thee,
    And thick darkness under thee;
Before me goeth a light,
    Behind me a sword;
Shall a remnant find grace in my sight?
    I am the Lord.

SIXTH ANTIPHONE

From all our lovers that love us
    Thou God didst sunder us;
Thou madest darkness above us,

And thick darkness under us;
Thou hast kindled thy wrath for a light,
    And made ready thy sword;
Let a remnant find grace in thy sight,
    We beseech thee, O Lord.

SEVENTH ANTIPHONE

Wilt thou bring fine gold for a payment
    For sins on this wise?
For the glittering of raiment
    And the shining of eyes,
For the painting of faces
    And the sundering of trust,
For the sins of thine high places
    And delight of thy lust?

For your high things ye shall have lowly,
    Lamentation for song;
For, behold, I God am holy,
    I the Lord am strong;
Ye shall seek me and shall not reach me
    Till the wine-press be trod;
In that hour ye shall turn and beseech me,
    Saith the Lord God.

EIGHTH ANTIPHONE

Not with fine gold for a payment,
    But with coin of sighs,
But with rending of raiment
    And with weeping of eyes,
But with shame of stricken faces
    And with strewing of dust,

For the sin of stately places
　And lordship of lust;

With voices of men made lowly,
　Made empty of song,
O Lord God most holy,
　O God most strong,
We reach out hands to reach thee
　Ere the wine-press be trod;
We beseech thee, O Lord, we beseech thee,
　O Lord our God.

NINTH ANTIPHONE

In that hour thou shalt say to the night,
　Come down and cover us;
To the cloud on thy left and thy right,
　Be thou spread over us;
A snare shall be as thy mother,
　And a curse thy bride;
Thou shalt put her away, and another
　Shall lie by thy side.

Thou shalt neither rise up by day
　Nor lie down by night;
Would God it were dark! thou shalt say;
　Would God it were light!
And the sight of thine eyes shall be made
　As the burning of fire;
And thy soul shall be sorely afraid
　For thy soul's desire.

Ye whom your lords loved well,
　Putting silver and gold on you,
The inevitable hell

Shall surely take hold on you;
Your gold shall be for a token,
    Your staff for a rod;
With the breaking of bands ye are broken,
    Saith the Lord God.

TENTH ANTIPHONE

In our sorrow we said to the night,
    Fall down and cover us;
To the darkness at left and at right,
    Be thou shed over us;
We had breaking of spirit to mother
    And cursing to bride;
And one was slain, and another
    Stood up at our side.

We could not arise by day,
    Nor lie down by night;
Thy sword was sharp in our way,
    Thy word in our sight;
The delight of our eyelids was made
    As the burning of fire;
And our souls became sorely afraid
    For our soul's desire.

We whom the world loved well,
    Laying silver and gold on us,
The kingdom of death and of hell
    Riseth up to take hold on us;
Our gold is turned to a token,
    Our staff to a rod;
Yet shalt thou bind them up that were broken,
    O Lord our God.

A LAMENTATION

Who hath known the ways of time
 Or trodden behind his feet?
  There is no such man among men.
For chance overcomes him, or crime
 Changes; for all things sweet
  In time wax bitter again.
Who shall give sorrow enough,
 Or who the abundance of tears?
Mine eyes are heavy with love
 And a sword gone thorough mine ears,
  A sound like a sword and fire,
  For pity, for great desire;
Who shall ensure me thereof,
 Lest I die, being full of my fears?

Who hath known the ways and the wrath,
 The sleepless spirit, the root
  And blossom of evil will,
   The divine device of a god?
Who shall behold it or hath?
 The twice-tongued prophets are mute,
  The many speakers are still;
   No foot has travelled or trod,
No hand has meted, his path.
 Man's fate is a blood-red fruit,
  And the mighty gods have their fill
  And relax not the rein, or the rod.

Ye were mighty in heart from of old,
 Ye slew with the spear, and are slain.
Keen after heat is the cold,
 Sore after summer is rain,
And melteth man to the bone.
 As water he weareth away,

As a flower, as an hour in a day,
Fallen from laughter to moan.
But my spirit is shaken with fear
  Lest an evil thing begin,
New-born, a spear for a spear,
  And one for another sin.
Or ever our tears began,
  It was known from of old and said;
One law for a living man,
  And another law for the dead.
For these are fearful and sad,
  Vain, and things without breath;
    While he lives let a man be glad,
      For none hath joy of his death.

Who hath known the pain, the old pain of earth,
  Or all the travail of the sea,
The many ways and waves, the birth
Fruitless, the labour nothing worth?
  Who hath known, who knoweth, O gods? not we.
There is none shall say he hath seen,
  There is none he hath known.
Though he saith, Lo, a lord have I been,
  I have reaped and sown;
I have seen the desire of mine eyes,
  The beginning of love,
The season of kisses and sighs
  And the end thereof.
I have known the ways of the sea,
  All the perilous ways,
Strange winds have spoken with me,
  And the tongues of strange days.
I have hewn the pine for ships;
  Where steeds run arow,
I have seen from their bridled lips
  Foam blown as the snow.

With snapping of chariot-poles
  And with straining of oars
I have grazed in the race the goals,
  In the storm the shores;
As a greave is cleft with an arrow
  At the joint of the knee,
I have cleft through the sea-straits narrow
  To the heart of the sea.
When air was smitten in sunder
  I have watched on high
The ways of the stars and the thunder
  In the night of the sky;
Where the dark brings forth light as a flower,
  As from lips that dissever;
One abideth the space of an hour,
  One endureth for ever.
Lo, what hath he seen or known,
  Of the way and the wave
Unbeholden, unsailed on, unsown,
  From the breast to the grave?

Or ever the stars were made, or skies,
  Grief was born, and the kinless night,
    Mother of gods without form or name.
And light is born out of heaven and dies,
  And one day knows not another's light,
    But night is one, and her shape the same.

But dumb the goddesses underground
  Wait, and we hear not on earth if their feet
    Rise, and the night wax loud with their wings;
Dumb, without word or shadow of sound;
  And sift in scales and winnow as wheat
    Men's souls, and sorrow of manifold things.

Nor less of grief than ours

The gods wrought long ago
  To bruise men one by one;
But with the incessant hours
  Fresh grief and greener woe
    Spring, as the sudden sun
Year after year makes flowers;
  And these die down and grow,
    And the next year lacks none.

As these men sleep, have slept
  The old heroes in time fled,
    No dream-divided sleep;
And holier eyes have wept
  Than ours, when on her dead
    Gods have seen Thetis weep,
With heavenly hair far-swept
  Back, heavenly hands outspread
    Round what she could not keep,

Could not one day withhold,
  One night; and like as these
    White ashes of no weight,
Held not his urn the cold
  Ashes of Heracles?
    For all things born one gate
Opens, no gate of gold;
  Opens; and no man sees
    Beyond the gods and fate.

ANIMA ANCEPS

Till death have broken
Sweet life's love-token,
Till all be spoken
  That shall be said,
What dost thou praying,
O soul, and playing
With song and saying,
  Things flown and fled?
For this we know not--
That fresh springs flow not
And fresh griefs grow not
  When men are dead;
When strange years cover
Lover and lover,
And joys are over
  And tears are shed.

If one day's sorrow
Mar the day's morrow--
If man's life borrow
  And man's death pay--
If souls once taken,
If lives once shaken,
Arise, awaken,
  By night, by day--
Why with strong crying
And years of sighing,
Living and dying,
  Fast ye and pray?
For all your weeping,
Waking and sleeping,
Death comes to reaping
  And takes away.

Though time rend after
Roof-tree from rafter,
A little laughter
  Is much more worth
Than thus to measure
The hour, the treasure,
The pain, the pleasure,
  The death, the birth;
Grief, when days alter,
Like joy shall falter;
Song-book and psalter,
  Mourning and mirth.
Live like the swallow;
Seek not to follow
Where earth is hollow
  Under the earth.

IN THE ORCHARD

(PROVENÇAL BURDEN)

Leave go my hands, let me catch breath and see;
Let the dew-fall drench either side of me;
Clear apple-leaves are soft upon that moon
Seen sidelong like a blossom in the tree;
Ah God, ah God, that day should be so soon.

The grass is thick and cool, it lets us lie.
Kissed upon either cheek and either eye,
I turn to thee as some green afternoon
Turns toward sunset, and is loth to die;
Ah God, ah God, that day should be so soon.

Lie closer, lean your face upon my side,
Feel where the dew fell that has hardly dried,
Hear how the blood beats that went nigh to swoon;
The pleasure lives there when the sense has died;
Ah God, ah God, that day should be so soon.

O my fair lord, I charge you leave me this:
Is it not sweeter than a foolish kiss?
Nay take it then, my flower, my first in June,
My rose, so like a tender mouth it is:
Ah God, ah God, that day should be so soon.

Love, till dawn sunder night from day with fire,
Dividing my delight and my desire,
The crescent life and love the plenilune,
Love me though dusk begin and dark retire;
Ah God, ah God, that day should be so soon.

Ah, my heart fails, my blood draws back; I know,
When life runs over, life is near to go;

And with the slain of love love's ways are strewn,
And with their blood, if love will have it so;
Ah God, ah God, that day should be so soon.

Ah, do thy will now; slay me if thou wilt;
There is no building now the walls are built,
No quarrying now the corner-stone is hewn,
No drinking now the vine's whole blood is spilt;
Ah God, ah God, that day should be so soon.

Nay, slay me now; nay, for I will be slain;
Pluck thy red pleasure from the teeth of pain,
Break down thy vine ere yet grape-gatherers prune,
Slay me ere day can slay desire again;
Ah God, ah God, that day should be so soon.

Yea, with thy sweet lips, with thy sweet sword; yea,
Take life and all, for I will die, I say;
Love, I gave love, is life a better boon?
For sweet night's sake I will not live till day;
Ah God, ah God, that day should be so soon.

Nay, I will sleep then only; nay, but go.
Ah sweet, too sweet to me, my sweet, I know
Love, sleep, and death go to the sweet same tune;
Hold my hair fast, and kiss me through it so.
Ah God, ah God, that day should be so soon.

A MATCH

If love were what the rose is,
  And I were like the leaf,
Our lives would grow together
In sad or singing weather,
Blown fields or flowerful closes,
  Green pleasure or grey grief;
If love were what the rose is,
  And I were like the leaf.

If I were what the words are,
  And love were like the tune,
With double sound and single
Delight our lips would mingle,
With kisses glad as birds are
  That get sweet rain at noon;
If I were what the words are,
  And love were like the tune.

If you were life, my darling,
  And I your love were death,
We'd shine and snow together
Ere March made sweet the weather
With daffodil and starling
  And hours of fruitful breath;
If you were life, my darling,
  And I your love were death.

If you were thrall to sorrow,
  And I were page to joy,
We'd play for lives and seasons
With loving looks and treasons
And tears of night and morrow
  And laughs of maid and boy;
If you were thrall to sorrow,

  And I were page to joy.

If you were April's lady,
  And I were lord in May,
We'd throw with leaves for hours
And draw for days with flowers,
Till day like night were shady
  And night were bright like day;
If you were April's lady,
  And I were lord in May.

If you were queen of pleasure,
  And I were king of pain,
We'd hunt down love together,
Pluck out his flying-feather,
And teach his feet a measure,
  And find his mouth a rein;
If you were queen of pleasure,
  And I were king of pain.

FAUSTINE

Ave Faustina Imperatrix, morituri te salutant.

Lean back, and get some minutes' peace;
  Let your head lean
Back to the shoulder with its fleece
  Of locks, Faustine.

The shapely silver shoulder stoops,
  Weighed over clean
With state of splendid hair that droops
  Each side, Faustine.

Let me go over your good gifts
  That crown you queen;
A queen whose kingdom ebbs and shifts
  Each week, Faustine.

Bright heavy brows well gathered up:
  White gloss and sheen;
Carved lips that make my lips a cup
  To drink, Faustine,

Wine and rank poison, milk and blood,
  Being mixed therein
Since first the devil threw dice with God
  For you, Faustine.

Your naked new-born soul, their stake,
  Stood blind between;
God said "let him that wins her take
  And keep Faustine."
But this time Satan throve, no doubt;
  Long since, I ween,
God's part in you was battered out;

Long since, Faustine.

The die rang sideways as it fell,
  Rang cracked and thin,
Like a man's laughter heard in hell
  Far down, Faustine,

A shadow of laughter like a sigh,
  Dead sorrow's kin;
So rang, thrown down, the devil's die
  That won Faustine.

A suckling of his breed you were,
  One hard to wean;
But God, who lost you, left you fair,
  We see, Faustine.

You have the face that suits a woman
  For her soul's screen--
The sort of beauty that's called human
  In hell, Faustine.

You could do all things but be good
  Or chaste of mien;
And that you would not if you could,
  We know, Faustine.

Even he who cast seven devils out
  Of Magdalene
Could hardly do as much, I doubt,
  For you, Faustine.

Did Satan make you to spite God?
  Or did God mean
To scourge with scorpions for a rod
  Our sins, Faustine?

I know what queen at first you were,
  As though I had seen
Red gold and black imperious hair
  Twice crown Faustine.

As if your fed sarcophagus
  Spared flesh and skin,
You come back face to face with us,
  The same Faustine.

She loved the games men played with death,
  Where death must win;
As though the slain man's blood and breath
  Revived Faustine.

Nets caught the pike, pikes tore the net;
  Lithe limbs and lean
From drained-out pores dripped thick red sweat
  To soothe Faustine.

She drank the steaming drift and dust
  Blown off the scene;
Blood could not ease the bitter lust
  That galled Faustine.

All round the foul fat furrows reeked,
  Where blood sank in;
The circus splashed and seethed and shrieked
  All round Faustine.

But these are gone now: years entomb
  The dust and din;
Yea, even the bath's fierce reek and fume
  That slew Faustine.

Was life worth living then? and now
  Is life worth sin?
Where are the imperial years? and how
  Are you Faustine?

Your soul forgot her joys, forgot
  Her times of teen;
Yea, this life likewise will you not
  Forget, Faustine?

For in the time we know not of
  Did fate begin
Weaving the web of days that wove
  Your doom, Faustine.

The threads were wet with wine, and all
  Were smooth to spin;
They wove you like a Bacchanal,
  The first Faustine.

And Bacchus cast your mates and you
  Wild grapes to glean;
Your flower-like lips were dashed with dew
  From his, Faustine.

Your drenched loose hands were stretched to hold
  The vine's wet green,
Long ere they coined in Roman gold
  Your face, Faustine.

Then after change of soaring feather
  And winnowing fin,
You woke in weeks of feverish weather,
  A new Faustine.

A star upon your birthday burned,

Whose fierce serene
Red pulseless planet never yearned
In heaven, Faustine.

Stray breaths of Sapphic song that blew
Through Mitylene
Shook the fierce quivering blood in you
By night, Faustine.

The shameless nameless love that makes
Hell's iron gin
Shut on you like a trap that breaks
The soul, Faustine.

And when your veins were void and dead,
What ghosts unclean
Swarmed round the straitened barren bed
That hid Faustine?

What sterile growths of sexless root
Or epicene?
What flower of kisses without fruit
Of love, Faustine?

What adders came to shed their coats?
What coiled obscene
Small serpents with soft stretching throats
Caressed Faustine?
But the time came of famished hours,
Maimed loves and mean,
This ghastly thin-faced time of ours,
To spoil Faustine.

You seem a thing that hinges hold,
A love-machine
With clockwork joints of supple gold--

No more, Faustine.

Not godless, for you serve one God,
  The Lampsacene,
Who metes the gardens with his rod;
  Your lord, Faustine.

If one should love you with real love
  (Such things have been,
Things your fair face knows nothing of,
  It seems, Faustine);

That clear hair heavily bound back,
  The lights wherein
Shift from dead blue to burnt-up black;
  Your throat, Faustine,

Strong, heavy, throwing out the face
  And hard bright chin
And shameful scornful lips that grace
  Their shame, Faustine,

Curled lips, long-since half kissed away,
  Still sweet and keen;
You'd give him--poison shall we say?
  Or what, Faustine?

A CAMEO

There was a graven image of Desire
    Painted with red blood on a ground of gold
    Passing between the young men and the old,
And by him Pain, whose body shone like fire,
And Pleasure with gaunt hands that grasped their hire.
    Of his left wrist, with fingers clenched and cold,
    The insatiable Satiety kept hold,
Walking with feet unshod that pashed the mire.
The senses and the sorrows and the sins,
    And the strange loves that suck the breasts of Hate
Till lips and teeth bite in their sharp indenture,
Followed like beasts with flap of wings and fins.
    Death stood aloof behind a gaping grate,
Upon whose lock was written _Peradventure_.

SONG BEFORE DEATH

(FROM THE FRENCH)

1795

  Sweet mother, in a minute's span
    Death parts thee and my love of thee;
  Sweet love, that yet art living man,
    Come back, true love, to comfort me.
  Back, ah, come back! ah wellaway!
  But my love comes not any day.

  As roses, when the warm West blows,
    Break to full flower and sweeten spring,
  My soul would break to a glorious rose
    In such wise at his whispering.
  In vain I listen; wellaway!
  My love says nothing any day.

  You that will weep for pity of love
    On the low place where I am lain,
  I pray you, having wept enough,
    Tell him for whom I bore such pain
  That he was yet, ah! wellaway!
  My true love to my dying day.

ROCOCO

Take hands and part with laughter;
  Touch lips and part with tears;
Once more and no more after,
  Whatever comes with years.
We twain shall not remeasure
  The ways that left us twain;
Nor crush the lees of pleasure
  From sanguine grapes of pain.

We twain once well in sunder,
  What will the mad gods do
For hate with me, I wonder,
  Or what for love with you?
Forget them till November,
  And dream there's April yet;
Forget that I remember,
  And dream that I forget.

Time found our tired love sleeping,
  And kissed away his breath;
But what should we do weeping,
  Though light love sleep to death?
We have drained his lips at leisure,
  Till there's not left to drain
A single sob of pleasure,
  A single pulse of pain.

Dream that the lips once breathless
  Might quicken if they would;
Say that the soul is deathless;
  Dream that the gods are good;
Say March may wed September,
  And time divorce regret;
But not that you remember,

And not that I forget.

We have heard from hidden places
  What love scarce lives and hears:
We have seen on fervent faces
  The pallor of strange tears:
We have trod the wine-vat's treasure,
  Whence, ripe to steam and stain,
Foams round the feet of pleasure
  The blood-red must of pain.

Remembrance may recover
  And time bring back to time
The name of your first lover,
  The ring of my first rhyme;
But rose-leaves of December
  The frosts of June shall fret,
The day that you remember,
  The day that I forget.

The snake that hides and hisses
  In heaven we twain have known;
The grief of cruel kisses,
  The joy whose mouth makes moan;
The pulse's pause and measure,
  Where in one furtive vein
Throbs through the heart of pleasure
  The purpler blood of pain.

We have done with tears and treasons
  And love for treason's sake;
Room for the swift new seasons,
  The years that burn and break,
Dismantle and dismember
  Men's days and dreams, Juliette;
For love may not remember,

But time will not forget.

Life treads down love in flying,
　Time withers him at root;
Bring all dead things and dying,
　Reaped sheaf and ruined fruit,
Where, crushed by three days' pressure,
　Our three days' love lies slain;
And earlier leaf of pleasure,
　And latter flower of pain.

Breathe close upon the ashes,
　It may be flame will leap;
Unclose the soft close lashes,
　Lift up the lids, and weep.
Light love's extinguished ember,
　Let one tear leave it wet
For one that you remember
　And ten that you forget.

STAGE LOVE

When the game began between them for a jest,
He played king and she played queen to match the best;
Laughter soft as tears, and tears that turned to laughter,
These were things she sought for years and sorrowed after.

Pleasure with dry lips, and pain that walks by night;
All the sting and all the stain of long delight;
These were things she knew not of, that knew not of her,
When she played at half a love with half a lover.

Time was chorus, gave them cues to laugh or cry;
They would kill, befool, amuse him, let him die;
Set him webs to weave to-day and break to-morrow,
Till he died for good in play, and rose in sorrow.

What the years mean; how time dies and is not slain;
How love grows and laughs and cries and wanes again;
These were things she came to know, and take their measure,
When the play was played out so for one man's pleasure.

...EPER

...g is better, I well think,
  Than love; the hidden well-water
Is not so delicate to drink:
  This was well seen of me and her.

I served her in a royal house;
  I served her wine and curious meat.
For will to kiss between her brows,
  I had no heart to sleep or eat.

Mere scorn God knows she had of me,
  A poor scribe, nowise great or fair,
Who plucked his clerk's hood back to see
  Her curled-up lips and amorous hair.

I vex my head with thinking this.
  Yea, though God always hated me,
And hates me now that I can kiss
  Her eyes, plait up her hair to see

How she then wore it on the brows,
  Yet am I glad to have her dead
Here in this wretched wattled house
  Where I can kiss her eyes and head.

Nothing is better, I well know,
  Than love; no amber in cold sea
Or gathered berries under snow:
  That is well seen of her and me.

Three thoughts I make my pleasure of:
  First I take heart and think of this:
That knight's gold hair she chose to love,
  His mouth she had such will to kiss.

Then I remember that sundawn
  I brought him by a privy way
Out at her lattice, and thereon
  What gracious words she found to say.

(Cold rushes for such little feet--
  Both feet could lie into my hand.
A marvel was it of my sweet
  Her upright body could so stand.)

"Sweet friend, God give you thank and grace;
  Now am I clean and whole of shame,
Nor shall men burn me in the face
  For my sweet fault that scandals them."

I tell you over word by word.
  She, sitting edgewise on her bed,
Holding her feet, said thus. The third,
  A sweeter thing than these, I said.

God, that makes time and ruins it
  And alters not, abiding God,
Changed with disease her body sweet,
  The body of love wherein she abode.

Love is more sweet and comelier
  Than a dove's throat strained out to sing.
All they spat out and cursed at her
  And cast her forth for a base thing.

They cursed her, seeing how God had wrought
  This curse to plague her, a curse of his.
Fools were they surely, seeing not
  How sweeter than all sweet she is.

He that had held her by the hair,
  With kissing lips blinding her eyes,
Felt her bright bosom, strained and bare,
  Sigh under him, with short mad cries

Out of her throat and sobbing mouth
  And body broken up with love,
With sweet hot tears his lips were loth
  Her own should taste the savour of,

Yea, he inside whose grasp all night
  Her fervent body leapt or lay,
Stained with sharp kisses red and white,
  Found her a plague to spurn away.

I hid her in this wattled house,
  I served her water and poor bread.
For joy to kiss between her brows
  Time upon time I was nigh dead.

Bread failed; we got but well-water
  And gathered grass with dropping seed.
I had such joy of kissing her,
  I had small care to sleep or feed.

Sometimes when service made me glad
  The sharp tears leapt between my lids,
Falling on her, such joy I had
  To do the service God forbids.

"I pray you let me be at peace,
  Get hence, make room for me to die."
She said that: her poor lip would cease,
  Put up to mine, and turn to cry.

I said, "Bethink yourself how love

Fared in us twain, what either did;
Shall I unclothe my soul thereof?
  That I should do this, God forbid."

Yea, though God hateth us, he knows
  That hardly in a little thing
Love faileth of the work it does
  Till it grow ripe for gathering.

Six months, and now my sweet is dead
  A trouble takes me; I know not
If all were done well, all well said,
  No word or tender deed forgot.

Too sweet, for the least part in her,
  To have shed life out by fragments; yet,
Could the close mouth catch breath and stir,
  I might see something I forget.

Six months, and I sit still and hold
  In two cold palms her cold two feet.
Her hair, half grey half ruined gold,
  Thrills me and burns me in kissing it.

Love bites and stings me through, to see
  Her keen face made of sunken bones.
Her worn-off eyelids madden me,
  That were shot through with purple once.

She said, "Be good with me; I grow
  So tired for shame's sake, I shall die
If you say nothing:" even so.
  And she is dead now, and shame put by.

Yea, and the scorn she had of me
  In the old time, doubtless vexed her then.

I never should have kissed her. See
  What fools God's anger makes of men!

She might have loved me a little too,
  Had I been humbler for her sake.
But that new shame could make love new
  She saw not--yet her shame did make.

I took too much upon my love,
  Having for such mean service done
Her beauty and all the ways thereof,
  Her face and all the sweet thereon.

Yea, all this while I tended her,
  I know the old love held fast his part:
I know the old scorn waxed heavier,
  Mixed with sad wonder, in her heart.

It may be all my love went wrong--
  A scribe's work writ awry and blurred,
Scrawled after the blind evensong--
  Spoilt music with no perfect word.

But surely I would fain have done
  All things the best I could. Perchance
Because I failed, came short of one,
  She kept at heart that other man's.

I am grown blind with all these things:
  It may be now she hath in sight
Some better knowledge; still there clings
  The old question. Will not God do right?[3]

[3] En ce temps-là estoyt dans ce pays grand nombre de ladres et de meseaulx, ce dont le roy eut grand desplaisir, veu que Dieu dust en estre moult griefvement courroucé.

Ores il advint qu'une noble damoyselle appelée Yolande de Sallières estant atteincte et touste guastée de ce vilain mal, tous ses amys et ses parens ayant devant leurs yeux la paour de Dieu la firent issir fors de leurs maisons et oncques ne voulurent recepvoir ni reconforter chose mauldicte de Dieu et à tous les hommes puante et abhominable. Ceste dame avoyt esté moult belle et gracieuse de formes, et de son corps elle estoyt large et de vie lascive. Pourtant nul des amans qui l'avoyent souventesfois accollée et baisée moult tendrement ne voulust plus héberger si laide femme et si détestable pescheresse. Ung seul clerc qui feut premièrement son lacquays et son entremetteur en matière d'amour la reçut chez luy et la récéla dans une petite cabane. Là mourut la meschinette de grande misère et de male mort: et après elle décéda ledist clerc qui pour grand amour l'avoyt six mois durant soignée, lavée, habillée et deshabillée tous les jours de ses mains propres. Mesme dist-on que ce meschant homme et mauldict clerc se remémourant de la grande beauté passée et guastée de ceste femme se délectoyt maintesfois à la baiser sur sa bouche orde et lépreuse et l'accoller doulcement de ses mains amoureuses. Aussy est-il mort de ceste mesme maladie abhominable. Cecy advint près Fontainebellant en Gastinois. Et quand ouyt le roy Philippe ceste adventure moult en estoyt esmerveillé.

Grandes Chroniques de France, 1505._

A BALLAD OF BURDENS

The burden of fair women. Vain delight,
  And love self-slain in some sweet shameful way,
And sorrowful old age that comes by night
  As a thief comes that has no heart by day,
  And change that finds fair cheeks and leaves them grey,
And weariness that keeps awake for hire,
  And grief that says what pleasure used to say;
This is the end of every man's desire.

The burden of bought kisses. This is sore,
  A burden without fruit in childbearing;
Between the nightfall and the dawn threescore,
  Threescore between the dawn and evening.
  The shuddering in thy lips, the shuddering
In thy sad eyelids tremulous like fire,
  Makes love seem shameful and a wretched thing,
This is the end of every man's desire.

The burden of sweet speeches. Nay, kneel down,
  Cover thy head, and weep; for verily
These market-men that buy thy white and brown
  In the last days shall take no thought for thee.
  In the last days like earth thy face shall be,
Yea, like sea-marsh made thick with brine and mire,
  Sad with sick leavings of the sterile sea.
This is the end of every man's desire.

The burden of long living. Thou shalt fear
  Waking, and sleeping mourn upon thy bed;
And say at night "Would God the day were here,"
  And say at dawn "Would God the day were dead."
  With weary days thou shalt be clothed and fed,
And wear remorse of heart for thine attire,
  Pain for thy girdle and sorrow upon thine head;

This is the end of every man's desire.

The burden of bright colours. Thou shalt see
  Gold tarnished, and the grey above the green;
And as the thing thou seest thy face shall be,
  And no more as the thing beforetime seen.
  And thou shalt say of mercy "It hath been,"
And living, watch the old lips and loves expire,
  And talking, tears shall take thy breath between;
This is the end of every man's desire.

The burden of sad sayings. In that day
  Thou shalt tell all thy days and hours, and tell
Thy times and ways and words of love, and say
  How one was dear and one desirable,
  And sweet was life to hear and sweet to smell,
But now with lights reverse the old hours retire
  And the last hour is shod with fire from hell;
This is the end of every man's desire.

The burden of four seasons. Rain in spring,
  White rain and wind among the tender trees;
A summer of green sorrows gathering,
  Rank autumn in a mist of miseries,
  With sad face set towards the year, that sees
The charred ash drop out of the dropping pyre,
  And winter wan with many maladies;
This is the end of every man's desire.

The burden of dead faces. Out of sight
  And out of love, beyond the reach of hands,
Changed in the changing of the dark and light,
  They walk and weep about the barren lands
  Where no seed is nor any garner stands,
Where in short breaths the doubtful days respire,
  And time's turned glass lets through the sighing sands;

This is the end of every man's desire.

The burden of much gladness. Life and lust
  Forsake thee, and the face of thy delight;
And underfoot the heavy hour strews dust,
  And overhead strange weathers burn and bite;
  And where the red was, lo the bloodless white,
And where truth was, the likeness of a liar,
  And where day was, the likeness of the night;
This is the end of every man's desire.

L'ENVOY

Princes, and ye whom pleasure quickeneth,
  Heed well this rhyme before your pleasure tire;
For life is sweet, but after life is death.
  This is the end of every man's desire.

RONDEL

Kissing her hair I sat against her feet,
Wove and unwove it, wound and found it sweet;
Made fast therewith her hands, drew down her eyes,
Deep as deep flowers and dreamy like dim skies;
With her own tresses bound and found her fair,
   Kissing her hair.

Sleep were no sweeter than her face to me,
Sleep of cold sea-bloom under the cold sea;
What pain could get between my face and hers?
What new sweet thing would love not relish worse?
Unless, perhaps, white death had kissed me there,
   Kissing her hair?

BEFORE THE MIRROR

(VERSES WRITTEN UNDER A PICTURE)

INSCRIBED TO J. A. WHISTLER

White rose in red rose-garden
  Is not so white;
Snowdrops that plead for pardon
  And pine for fright
Because the hard East blows
Over their maiden rows
  Grow not as this face grows from pale to bright.

Behind the veil, forbidden,
  Shut up from sight,
Love, is there sorrow hidden,
  Is there delight?
Is joy thy dower or grief,
White rose of weary leaf,
  Late rose whose life is brief, whose loves are light?

Soft snows that hard winds harden
  Till each flake bite
Fill all the flowerless garden
  Whose flowers took flight
Long since when summer ceased,
And men rose up from feast,
  And warm west wind grew east, and warm day night.

"Come snow, come wind or thunder
  High up in air,
I watch my face, and wonder
  At my bright hair;
Nought else exalts or grieves
The rose at heart, that heaves

With love of her own leaves and lips that pair.

"She knows not loves that kissed her
  She knows not where.
Art thou the ghost, my sister,
  White sister there,
Am I the ghost, who knows?
My hand, a fallen rose,
  Lies snow-white on white snows, and takes no care.

"I cannot see what pleasures
  Or what pains were;
What pale new loves and treasures
  New years will bear;
What beam will fall, what shower,
What grief or joy for dower;
  But one thing-knows the flower; the flower is fair."

Glad, but not flushed with gladness,
  Since joys go by;
Sad, but not bent with sadness,
  Since sorrows die;
Deep in the gleaming glass
She sees all past things pass,
  And all sweet life that was lie down and lie.

There glowing ghosts of flowers
  Draw down, draw nigh;
And wings of swift spent hours
  Take flight and fly;
She sees by formless gleams,
She hears across cold streams,
  Dead mouths of many dreams that sing and sigh.

Face fallen and white throat lifted,
  With sleepless eye

She sees old loves that drifted,
  She knew not why,
Old loves and faded fears
Float down a stream that hears
  The flowing of all men's tears beneath the sky.

EROTION

Sweet for a little even to fear, and sweet,
O love, to lay down fear at love's fair feet;
Shall not some fiery memory of his breath
Lie sweet on lips that touch the lips of death?
Yet leave me not; yet, if thou wilt, be free;
Love me no more, but love my love of thee.
Love where thou wilt, and live thy life; and I,
One thing I can, and one love cannot--die.
Pass from me; yet thine arms, thine eyes, thine hair,
Feed my desire and deaden my despair.
Yet once more ere time change us, ere my cheek
Whiten, ere hope be dumb or sorrow speak,
Yet once more ere thou hate me, one full kiss;
Keep other hours for others, save me this.
Yea, and I will not (if it please thee) weep,
Lest thou be sad; I will but sigh, and sleep.
Sweet, does death hurt? thou canst not do me wrong:
I shall not lack thee, as I loved thee, long.
Hast thou not given me above all that live
Joy, and a little sorrow shalt not give?
What even though fairer fingers of strange girls
Pass nestling through thy beautiful boy's curls
As mine did, or those curled lithe lips of thine
Meet theirs as these, all theirs come after mine;
And though I were not, though I be not, best,
I have loved and love thee more than all the rest.
O love, O lover, loose or hold me fast,
I had thee first, whoever have thee last;
Fairer or not, what need I know, what care?
To thy fair bud my blossom once seemed fair.
Why am I fair at all before thee, why
At all desired? seeing thou art fair, not I.
I shall be glad of thee, O fairest head,
Alive, alone, without thee, with thee, dead;

I shall remember while the light lives yet,
And in the night-time I shall not forget.
Though (as thou wilt) thou leave me ere life leave,
I will not, for thy love I will not, grieve;
Not as they use who love not more than I,
Who love not as I love thee though I die;
And though thy lips, once mine, be oftener prest
To many another brow and balmier breast,
And sweeter arms, or sweeter to thy mind,
Lull thee or lure, more fond thou wilt not find.

IN MEMORY OF WALTER SAVAGE LANDOR

Back to the flower-town, side by side,
   The bright months bring,
New-born, the bridegroom and the bride,
   Freedom and spring.

The sweet land laughs from sea to sea,
   Filled full of sun;
All things come back to her, being free;
   All things but one.

In many a tender wheaten plot
   Flowers that were dead
Live, and old suns revive; but not
   That holier head.

By this white wandering waste of sea,
   Far north, I hear
One face shall never turn to me
   As once this year:

Shall never smile and turn and rest
   On mine as there,
Nor one most sacred hand be prest
   Upon my hair.

I came as one whose thoughts half linger,
   Half run before;
The youngest to the oldest singer
   That England bore.

I found him whom I shall not find
   Till all grief end,
In holiest age our mightiest mind,
   Father and friend.

But thou, if anything endure,
   If hope there be,
O spirit that man's life left pure,
   Man's death set free,

Not with disdain of days that were
   Look earthward now;
Let dreams revive the reverend hair,
   The imperial brow;

Come back in sleep, for in the life
   Where thou art not
We find none like thee. Time and strife
   And the world's lot

Move thee no more; but love at least
   And reverent heart
May move thee, royal and released,
   Soul, as thou art.

And thou, his Florence, to thy trust
   Receive and keep,
Keep safe his dedicated dust,
   His sacred sleep.

So shall thy lovers, come from far,
   Mix with thy name
As morning-star with evening-star
   His faultless fame

A SONG IN TIME OF ORDER. 1852

Push hard across the sand,
    For the salt wind gathers breath;
Shoulder and wrist and hand,
    Push hard as the push of death.

The wind is as iron that rings,
    The foam-heads loosen and flee;
It swells and welters and swings,
    The pulse of the tide of the sea.

And up on the yellow cliff
    The long corn flickers and shakes;
Push, for the wind holds stiff,
    And the gunwale dips and rakes.

Good hap to the fresh fierce weather,
    The quiver and beat of the sea!
While three men hold together,
    The kingdoms are less by three.

Out to the sea with her there,
    Out with her over the sand;
Let the kings keep the earth for their share!
    We have done with the sharers of land.

They have tied the world in a tether,
    They have bought over God with a fee;
While three men hold together,
    The kingdoms are less by three.

We have done with the kisses that sting,
    The thief's mouth red from the feast,
The blood on the hands of the king
    And the lie at the lips of the priest.

Will they tie the winds in a tether,
  Put a bit in the jaws of the sea?
While three men hold together,
  The kingdoms are less by three.

Let our flag run out straight in the wind!
  The old red shall be floated again
When the ranks that are thin shall be thinned,
  When the names that were twenty are ten;

When the devil's riddle is mastered
  And the galley-bench creaks with a Pope,
We shall see Buonaparte the bastard
  Kick heels with his throat in a rope.

While the shepherd sets wolves on his sheep
  And the emperor halters his kine,
While Shame is a watchman asleep
  And Faith is a keeper of swine,

Let the wind shake our flag like a feather,
  Like the plumes of the foam of the sea!
While three men hold together,
  The kingdoms are less by three.

All the world has its burdens to bear,
  From Cayenne to the Austrian whips;
Forth, with the rain in our hair
  And the salt sweet foam in our lips;

In the teeth of the hard glad weather,
  In the blown wet face of the sea;
While three men hold together,
  The kingdoms are less by three.

A SONG IN TIME OF REVOLUTION. 1860

The heart of the rulers is sick, and the high-priest covers his head:
For this is the song of the quick that is heard in the ears of the dead.

The poor and the halt and the blind are keen and mighty and fleet:
Like the noise of the blowing of wind is the sound of the noise of their feet.

The wind has the sound of a laugh in the clamour of days and of deeds:
The priests are scattered like chaff, and the rulers broken like reeds.

The high-priest sick from qualms, with his raiment bloodily dashed;
The thief with branded palms, and the liar with cheeks abashed.

They are smitten, they tremble greatly, they are pained for their pleasant things:
For the house of the priests made stately, and the might in the mouth of the kings.

They are grieved and greatly afraid; they are taken, they shall not flee:
For the heart of the nations is made as the strength of the springs of the sea.

They were fair in the grace of gold, they walked with delicate feet:
They were clothed with the cunning of old, and the smell of their garments was sweet.

For the breaking of gold in their hair they halt as a man made lame:
They are utterly naked and bare; their mouths are bitter with shame.

Wilt thou judge thy people now, O king that wast found most wise?
Wilt thou lie any more, O thou whose mouth is emptied of lies?

Shall God make a pact with thee, till his hook be found in thy sides?
Wilt thou put back the time of the sea, or the place of the season of tides?

Set a word in thy lips, to stand before God with a word in thy mouth:
That "the rain shall return in the land, and the tender dew after drouth."

But the arm of the elders is broken, their strength is unbound and undone:
They wait for a sign of a token; they cry, and there cometh none.

Their moan is in every place, the cry of them filleth the land:
There is shame in the sight of their face, there is fear in the thews of their hand.

They are girdled about the reins with a curse for the girdle thereon:
For the noise of the rending of chains the face of their colour is gone.

For the sound of the shouting of men they are grievously stricken at heart:
They are smitten asunder with pain, their bones are smitten apart.

There is none of them all that is whole; their lips gape open for breath;
They are clothed with sickness of soul, and the shape of the shadow of death.

The wind is thwart in their feet; it is full of the shouting of mirth;
As one shaketh the sides of a sheet, so it shaketh the ends of the earth.

The sword, the sword is made keen; the iron has opened its mouth;
The corn is red that was green; it is bound for the sheaves of the south.

The sound of a word was shed, the sound of the wind as a breath,
In the ears of the souls that were dead, in the dust of the deepness of death;

Where the face of the moon is taken, the ways of the stars undone,
The light of the whole sky shaken, the light of the face of the sun:

Where the waters are emptied and broken, the waves of the waters are stayed;
Where God has bound for a token the darkness that maketh afraid;

Where the sword was covered and hidden, and dust had grown in its side,
A word came forth which was bidden, the crying of one that cried:

The sides of the two-edged sword shall be bare, and its mouth shall be red,
For the breath of the face of the Lord that is felt in the bones of the dead.

TO VICTOR HUGO

In the fair days when God
By man as godlike trod,
And each alike was Greek, alike was free,
God's lightning spared, they said,
Alone the happier head
Whose laurels screened it; fruitless grace for thee,
To whom the high gods gave of right
Their thunders and their laurels and their light.

Sunbeams and bays before
Our master's servants wore,
For these Apollo left in all men's lands;
But far from these ere now
And watched with jealous brow
Lay the blind lightnings shut between God's hands,
And only loosed on slaves and kings
The terror of the tempest of their wings.

Born in those younger years
That shone with storms of spears
And shook in the wind blown from a dead world's pyre,
When by her back-blown hair
Napoleon caught the fair
And fierce Republic with her feet of fire,
And stayed with iron words and hands
Her flight, and freedom in a thousand lands:

Thou sawest the tides of things
Close over heads of kings,
And thine hand felt the thunder, and to thee
Laurels and lightnings were
As sunbeams and soft air
Mixed each in other, or as mist with sea
Mixed, or as memory with desire,

Or the lute's pulses with the louder lyre.

  For thee man's spirit stood
  Disrobed of flesh and blood,
And bare the heart of the most secret hours;
  And to thine hand more tame
  Than birds in winter came
High hopes and unknown flying forms of powers,
  And from thy table fed, and sang
Till with the tune men's ears took fire and rang.

  Even all men's eyes and ears
  With fiery sound and tears
Waxed hot, and cheeks caught flame and eyelid light,
  At those high songs of thine
  That stung the sense like wine,
Or fell more soft than dew or snow by night,
  Or wailed as in some flooded cave
Sobs the strong broken spirit of a wave.

  But we, our master, we
  Whose hearts, uplift to thee,
Ache with the pulse of thy remembered song,
  We ask not nor await
  From the clenched hands of fate,
As thou, remission of the world's old wrong;
  Respite we ask not, nor release;
Freedom a man may have, he shall not peace.

  Though thy most fiery hope
  Storm heaven, to set wide ope
The all-sought-for gate whence God or Chance debars
  All feet of men, all eyes--
  The old night resumes her skies,
Her hollow hiding-place of clouds and stars,
  Where nought save these is sure in sight;

And, paven with death, our days are roofed with night.

  One thing we can; to be
  Awhile, as men may, free;
But not by hope or pleasure the most stern
  Goddess, most awful-eyed,
  Sits, but on either side
Sit sorrow and the wrath of hearts that burn,
  Sad faith that cannot hope or fear,
And memory grey with many a flowerless year.

  Not that in stranger's wise
  I lift not loving eyes
To the fair foster-mother France, that gave
  Beyond the pale fleet foam
  Help to my sires and home,
Whose great sweet breast could shelter those and save
  Whom from her nursing breasts and hands
Their land cast forth of old on gentler lands.

  Not without thoughts that ache
  For theirs and for thy sake,
I, born of exiles, hail thy banished head;
  I whose young song took flight
  Toward the great heat and light
On me a child from thy far splendour shed,
  From thine high place of soul and song,
Which, fallen on eyes yet feeble, made them strong.

  Ah, not with lessening love
  For memories born hereof,
I look to that sweet mother-land, and see
  The old fields and fair full streams,
  And skies, but fled like dreams
The feet of freedom and the thought of thee;
  And all between the skies and graves

The mirth of mockers and the shame of slaves.

  She, killed with noisome air,
  Even she! and still so fair,
Who said "Let there be freedom," and there was
  Freedom; and as a lance
  The fiery eyes of France
Touched the world's sleep and as a sleep made pass
  Forth of men's heavier ears and eyes
Smitten with fire and thunder from new skies.

  Are they men's friends indeed
  Who watch them weep and bleed?
Because thou hast loved us, shall the gods love thee?
  Thou, first of men and friend,
  Seest thou, even thou, the end?
Thou knowest what hath been, knowest thou what shall be?
  Evils may pass and hopes endure;
But fate is dim, and all the gods obscure.

  O nursed in airs apart,
  O poet highest of heart,
Hast thou seen time, who hast seen so many things?
  Are not the years more wise,
  More sad than keenest eyes,
The years with soundless feet and sounding wings?
  Passing we hear them not, but past
The clamour of them thrills us, and their blast.

Thou art chief of us, and lord;
  Thy song is as a sword
Keen-edged and scented in the blade from flowers;
  Thou art lord and king; but we
  Lift younger eyes, and see

Less of high hope, less light on wandering hours;
  Hours that have borne men down so long,
Seen the right fail, and watched uplift the wrong.

  But thine imperial soul,
  As years and ruins roll
To the same end, and all things and all dreams
  With the same wreck and roar
  Drift on the dim same shore,
Still in the bitter foam and brackish streams
  Tracks the fresh water-spring to be
And sudden sweeter fountains in the sea.

  As once the high God bound
  With many a rivet round
Man's saviour, and with iron nailed him through,
  At the wild end of things,
  Where even his own bird's wings
Flagged, whence the sea shone like a drop of dew,
  From Caucasus beheld below
Past fathoms of unfathomable snow;

  So the strong God, the chance
  Central of circumstance,
Still shows him exile who will not be slave;
  All thy great fame and thee
  Girt by the dim strait sea
With multitudinous walls of wandering wave;
  Shows us our greatest from his throne
Fate-stricken, and rejected of his own.

  Yea, he is strong, thou say'st,
  A mystery many-faced,
The wild beasts know him and the wild birds flee;
  The blind night sees him, death
  Shrinks beaten at his breath,

And his right hand is heavy on the sea:
  We know he hath made us, and is king;
We know not if he care for anything.

  Thus much, no more, we know;
  He bade what is be so,
Bade light be and bade night be, one by one;
  Bade hope and fear, bade ill
  And good redeem and kill,
Till all men be aweary of the sun
  And his world burn in its own flame
And bear no witness longer of his name.

  Yet though all this be thus,
  Be those men praised of us
Who have loved and wrought and sorrowed and not sinned
  For fame or fear or gold,
  Nor waxed for winter cold,
Nor changed for changes of the worldly wind;
  Praised above men of men be these,
Till this one world and work we know shall cease.

  Yea, one thing more than this,
  We know that one thing is,
The splendour of a spirit without blame,
  That not the labouring years
  Blind-born, nor any fears,
Nor men nor any gods can tire or tame;
  But purer power with fiery breath
Fills, and exalts above the gulfs of death.

  Praised above men be thou,
  Whose laurel-laden brow,
Made for the morning, droops not in the night;
  Praised and beloved, that none

  Of all thy great things done
Flies higher than thy most equal spirit's flight;
  Praised, that nor doubt nor hope could bend
Earth's loftiest head, found upright to the end.

BEFORE DAWN

Sweet life, if life were stronger,
Earth clear of years that wrong her,
Then two things might live longer,
  Two sweeter things than they;
Delight, the rootless flower,
And love, the bloomless bower;
Delight that lives an hour,
  And love that lives a day.

From evensong to daytime,
When April melts in Maytime,
Love lengthens out his playtime,
  Love lessens breath by breath,
And kiss by kiss grows older
On listless throat or shoulder
Turned sideways now, turned colder
  Than life that dreams of death.

This one thing once worth giving
Life gave, and seemed worth living;
Sin sweet beyond forgiving
  And brief beyond regret:
To laugh and love together
And weave with foam and feather
And wind and words the tether
  Our memories play with yet.

Ah, one thing worth beginning,
One thread in life worth spinning,
Ah sweet, one sin worth sinning
  With all the whole soul's will;
To lull you till one stilled you,
To kiss you till one killed you,
To feed you till one filled you,

Sweet lips, if love could fill;

To hunt sweet Love and lose him
Between white arms and bosom,
Between the bud and blossom,
  Between your throat and chin;
To say of shame--what is it?
Of virtue--we can miss it,
Of sin--we can but kiss it,
  And it's no longer sin:

To feel the strong soul, stricken
Through fleshly pulses, quicken
Beneath swift sighs that thicken,
  Soft hands and lips that smite;
Lips that no love can tire,
With hands that sting like fire,
Weaving the web Desire
  To snare the bird Delight.

But love so lightly plighted,
Our love with torch unlighted,
Paused near us unaffrighted,
  Who found and left him free;
None, seeing us cloven in sunder,
Will weep or laugh or wonder;
Light love stands clear of thunder,
  And safe from winds at sea.

As, when late larks give warning
Of dying lights and dawning,
Night murmurs to the morning,
  "Lie still, O love, lie still;"
And half her dark limbs cover
The white limbs of her lover,
With amorous plumes that hover

   And fervent lips that chill;

As scornful day represses
Night's void and vain caresses,
And from her cloudier tresses
  Unwinds the gold of his,
With limbs from limbs dividing
And breath by breath subsiding;
For love has no abiding,
  But dies before the kiss;

So hath it been, so be it;
For who shall live and flee it?
But look that no man see it
  Or hear it unaware;
Lest all who love and choose him
See Love, and so refuse him;
For all who find him lose him,
  But all have found him fair.

DOLORES

(NOTRE-DAME DES SEPT DOULEURS)

Cold eyelids that hide like a jewel
  Hard eyes that grow soft for an hour;
The heavy white limbs, and the cruel
  Red mouth like a venomous flower;
When these are gone by with their glories,
  What shall rest of thee then, what remain,
O mystic and sombre Dolores,
    Our Lady of Pain?

Seven sorrows the priests give their Virgin;
  But thy sins, which are seventy times seven,
Seven ages would fail thee to purge in,
  And then they would haunt thee in heaven:
Fierce midnights and famishing morrows,
  And the loves that complete and control
All the joys of the flesh, all the sorrows
    That wear out the soul.

O garment not golden but gilded,
  O garden where all men may dwell,
O tower not of ivory, but builded
  By hands that reach heaven from hell;
O mystical rose of the mire,
  O house not of gold but of gain,
O house of unquenchable fire,
    Our Lady of Pain!

O lips full of lust and of laughter,
  Curled snakes that are fed from my breast,
Bite hard, lest remembrance come after
  And press with new lips where you pressed.
For my heart too springs up at the pressure,

   Mine eyelids too moisten and burn;
Ah, feed me and fill me with pleasure,
   Ere pain come in turn.

In yesterday's reach and to-morrow's,
   Out of sight though they lie of to-day,
There have been and there yet shall be sorrows
   That smite not and bite not in play.
The life and the love thou despisest,
   These hurt us indeed, and in vain,
O wise among women, and wisest,
   Our Lady of Pain.

Who gave thee thy wisdom? what stories
   That stung thee, what visions that smote?
Wert thou pure and a maiden, Dolores,
   When desire took thee first by the throat?
What bud was the shell of a blossom
   That all men may smell to and pluck?
What milk fed thee first at what bosom?
   What sins gave thee suck?

We shift and bedeck and bedrape us,
   Thou art noble and nude and antique;
Libitina thy mother, Priapus
   Thy father, a Tuscan and Greek.
We play with light loves in the portal,
   And wince and relent and refrain;
Loves die, and we know thee immortal,
   Our Lady of Pain.

Fruits fail and love dies and time ranges;
   Thou art fed with perpetual breath,
And alive after infinite changes,
   And fresh from the kisses of death;
Of languors rekindled and rallied,

Of barren delights and unclean,
Things monstrous and fruitless, a pallid
  And poisonous queen.

Could you hurt me, sweet lips, though I hurt you?
  Men touch them, and change in a trice
The lilies and languors of virtue
  For the raptures and roses of vice;
Those lie where thy foot on the floor is,
  These crown and caress thee and chain,
O splendid and sterile Dolores,
  Our Lady of Pain.

There are sins it may be to discover,
  There are deeds it may be to delight.
What new work wilt thou find for thy lover,
  What new passions for daytime or night?
What spells that they know not a word of
  Whose lives are as leaves overblown?
What tortures undreamt of, unheard of,
  Unwritten, unknown?

Ah beautiful passionate body
  That never has ached with a heart!
On thy mouth though the kisses are bloody,
  Though they sting till it shudder and smart,
More kind than the love we adore is,
  They hurt not the heart or the brain,
O bitter and tender Dolores,
  Our Lady of Pain.

As our kisses relax and redouble,
  From the lips and the foam and the fangs
Shall no new sin be born for men's trouble,
  No dream of impossible pangs?
With the sweet of the sins of old ages

Wilt thou satiate thy soul as of yore?
Too sweet is the rind, say the sages,
  Too bitter the core.

Hast thou told all thy secrets the last time,
  And bared all thy beauties to one?
Ah, where shall we go then for pastime,
  If the worst that can be has been done?
But sweet as the rind was the core is;
  We are fain of thee still, we are fain,
O sanguine and subtle Dolores,
  Our Lady of Pain.

By the hunger of change and emotion,
  By the thirst of unbearable things,
By despair, the twin-born of devotion,
  By the pleasure that winces and stings,
The delight that consumes the desire,
  The desire that outruns the delight,
By the cruelty deaf as a fire
  And blind as the night,

By the ravenous teeth that have smitten
  Through the kisses that blossom and bud,
By the lips intertwisted and bitten
  Till the foam has a savour of blood,
By the pulse as it rises and falters,
  By the hands as they slacken and strain,

I adjure thee, respond from thine altars,
  Our Lady of Pain.

Wilt thou smile as a woman disdaining
  The light fire in the veins of a boy?
But he comes to thee sad, without feigning,
  Who has wearied of sorrow and joy;

Less careful of labour and glory
  Than the elders whose hair has uncurled;
And young, but with fancies as hoary
  And grey as the world.

I have passed from the outermost portal
  To the shrine where a sin is a prayer;
What care though the service be mortal?
  O our Lady of Torture, what care?
All thine the last wine that I pour is,
  The last in the chalice we drain,
O fierce and luxurious Dolores,
    Our Lady of Pain.

All thine the new wine of desire,
  The fruit of four lips as they clung
Till the hair and the eyelids took fire,
  The foam of a serpentine tongue,
The froth of the serpents of pleasure,
  More salt than the foam of the sea,
Now felt as a flame, now at leisure
  As wine shed for me.

Ah thy people, thy children, thy chosen,
  Marked cross from the womb and perverse!
They have found out the secret to cozen
  The gods that constrain us and curse;
They alone, they are wise, and none other;
  Give me place, even me, in their train,
O my sister, my spouse, and my mother,
    Our Lady of Pain.

For the crown of our life as it closes
  Is darkness, the fruit thereof dust;
No thorns go as deep as a rose's,
  And love is more cruel than lust.

Time turns the old days to derision,
  Our loves into corpses or wives;
And marriage and death and division
  Make barren our lives.

And pale from the past we draw nigh thee,
  And satiate with comfortless hours;
And we know thee, how all men belie thee,
  And we gather the fruit of thy flowers;
The passion that slays and recovers,
  The pangs and the kisses that rain
On the lips and the limbs of thy lovers,
  Our Lady of Pain.

The desire of thy furious embraces
  Is more than the wisdom of years,
On the blossom though blood lie in traces,
  Though the foliage be sodden with tears.
For the lords in whose keeping the door is
  That opens on all who draw breath
Gave the cypress to love, my Dolores,
  The myrtle to death.

And they laughed, changing hands in the measure,
  And they mixed and made peace after strife;
Pain melted in tears, and was pleasure;
  Death tingled with blood, and was life.
Like lovers they melted and tingled,
  In the dusk of thine innermost fane;
In the darkness they murmured and mingled,
  Our Lady of Pain.

In a twilight where virtues are vices,
  In thy chapels, unknown of the sun,
To a tune that enthralls and entices,
  They were wed, and the twain were as one.

For the tune from thine altar hath sounded
  Since God bade the world's work begin,
And the fume of thine incense abounded,
  To sweeten the sin.

Love listens, and paler than ashes,
  Through his curls as the crown on them slips,
Lifts languid wet eyelids and lashes,
  And laughs with insatiable lips.
Thou shalt hush him with heavy caresses,
  With music that scares the profane;
Thou shalt darken his eyes with thy tresses,
  Our Lady of Pain.

Thou shalt blind his bright eyes though he wrestle,
  Thou shalt chain his light limbs though he strive;
In his lips all thy serpents shall nestle,
  In his hands all thy cruelties thrive.
In the daytime thy voice shall go through him,
  In his dreams he shall feel thee and ache;
Thou shalt kindle by night and subdue him
  Asleep and awake.

Thou shalt touch and make redder his roses
  With juice not of fruit nor of bud;
When the sense in the spirit reposes,
  Thou shalt quicken the soul through the blood.
Thine, thine the one grace we implore is,
  Who would live and not languish or feign,
O sleepless and deadly Dolores,
  Our Lady of Pain.

Dost thou dream, in a respite of slumber,
  In a lull of the fires of thy life,
Of the days without name, without number,
  When thy will stung the world into strife;

When, a goddess, the pulse of thy passion
  Smote kings as they revelled in Rome;
And they hailed thee re-risen, O Thalassian,
  Foam-white, from the foam?

When thy lips had such lovers to flatter;
  When the city lay red from thy rods,
And thine hands were as arrows to scatter
  The children of change and their gods;
When the blood of thy foemen made fervent
  A sand never moist from the main,
As one smote them, their lord and thy servant,
  Our Lady of Pain.

On sands by the storm never shaken,
  Nor wet from the washing of tides;
Nor by foam of the waves overtaken,
  Nor winds that the thunder bestrides;
But red from the print of thy paces,
  Made smooth for the world and its lords,
Ringed round with a flame of fair faces,
  And splendid with swords.

There the gladiator, pale for thy pleasure,
  Drew bitter and perilous breath;
There torments laid hold on the treasure
  Of limbs too delicious for death;
When thy gardens were lit with live torches;
  When the world was a steed for thy rein;
When the nations lay prone in thy porches,
  Our Lady of Pain.

When, with flame all around him aspirant,
  Stood flushed, as a harp-player stands,
The implacable beautiful tyrant,
  Rose-crowned, having death in his hands;

And a sound as the sound of loud water
  Smote far through the flight of the fires,
And mixed with the lightning of slaughter
  A thunder of lyres.

Dost thou dream of what was and no more is,
  The old kingdoms of earth and the kings?
Dost thou hunger for these things, Dolores,
  For these, in a world of new things?
But thy bosom no fasts could emaciate,
  No hunger compel to complain
Those lips that no bloodshed could satiate,
  Our Lady of Pain.

As of old when the world's heart was lighter,
  Through thy garments the grace of thee glows,
The white wealth of thy body made whiter
  By the blushes of amorous blows,
And seamed with sharp lips and fierce fingers,
  And branded by kisses that bruise;
When all shall be gone that now lingers,
  Ah, what shall we lose?

Thou wert fair in the fearless old fashion,
  And thy limbs are as melodies yet,
And move to the music of passion
  With lithe and lascivious regret.
What ailed us, O gods, to desert you
  For creeds that refuse and restrain?
Come down and redeem us from virtue,
  Our Lady of Pain.

All shrines that were Vestal are flameless,
  But the flame has not fallen from this;
Though obscure be the god, and though nameless

The eyes and the hair that we kiss;
Low fires that love sits by and forges
  Fresh heads for his arrows and thine;
Hair loosened and soiled in mid orgies
  With kisses and wine.

Thy skin changes country and colour,
  And shrivels or swells to a snake's.
Let it brighten and bloat and grow duller,
  We know it, the flames and the flakes,
Red brands on it smitten and bitten,
  Round skies where a star is a stain,
And the leaves with thy litanies written,
  Our Lady of Pain.

On thy bosom though many a kiss be,
  There are none such as knew it of old.
Was it Alciphron once or Arisbe,
  Male ringlets or feminine gold,
That thy lips met with under the statue,
  Whence a look shot out sharp after thieves
From the eyes of the garden-god at you
  Across the fig-leaves?
Then still, through dry seasons and moister,
  One god had a wreath to his shrine;
Then love was the pearl of his oyster,[4]
  And Venus rose red out of wine.
We have all done amiss, choosing rather
  Such loves as the wise gods disdain;
Intercede for us thou with thy father,
  Our Lady of Pain.

In spring he had crowns of his garden,
  Red corn in the heat of the year,
Then hoary green olives that harden
  When the grape-blossom freezes with fear;

And milk-budded myrtles with Venus
  And vine-leaves with Bacchus he trod;
And ye said, "We have seen, he hath seen us,
  A visible God."

What broke off the garlands that girt you?
  What sundered you spirit and clay?
Weak sins yet alive are as virtue
  To the strength of the sins of that day.
For dried is the blood of thy lover,
  Ipsithilla, contracted the vein;
Cry aloud, "Will he rise and recover,
  Our Lady of Pain?"

Cry aloud; for the old world is broken:
  Cry out; for the Phrygian is priest,
And rears not the bountiful token
  And spreads not the fatherly feast.
From the midmost of Ida, from shady
Recesses that murmur at morn,
  They have brought and baptized her, Our Lady,
    A goddess new-born.

And the chaplets of old are above us,
  And the oyster-bed teems out of reach;
Old poets outsing and outlove us,
  And Catullus makes mouths at our speech.
Who shall kiss, in thy father's own city,
  With such lips as he sang with, again?
Intercede for us all of thy pity,
  Our Lady of Pain.

Out of Dindymus heavily laden
  Her lions draw bound and unfed
A mother, a mortal, a maiden,

A queen over death and the dead.
She is cold, and her habit is lowly,
  Her temple of branches and sods;
Most fruitful and virginal, holy,
  A mother of gods.

She hath wasted with fire thine high places,
  She hath hidden and marred and made sad
The fair limbs of the Loves, the fair faces
  Of gods that were goodly and glad.
She slays, and her hands are not bloody;
  She moves as a moon in the wane,
White-robed, and thy raiment is ruddy,
  Our Lady of Pain.

They shall pass and their places be taken,
  The gods and the priests that are pure.
They shall pass, and shalt thou not be shaken?
  They shall perish, and shalt thou endure?
Death laughs, breathing close and relentless
  In the nostrils and eyelids of lust,
With a pinch in his fingers of scentless
  And delicate dust.

But the worm shall revive thee with kisses;
  Thou shalt change and transmute as a god,
As the rod to a serpent that hisses,
  As the serpent again to a rod.
Thy life shall not cease though thou doff it;
  Thou shalt live until evil be slain,
And good shall die first, said thy prophet,
  Our Lady of Pain.

Did he lie? did he laugh? does he know it,
  Now he lies out of reach, out of breath,
Thy prophet, thy preacher, thy poet,

Sin's child by incestuous Death?
Did he find out in fire at his waking,
  Or discern as his eyelids lost light,
When the bands of the body were breaking
  And all came in sight?

Who has known all the evil before us,
  Or the tyrannous secrets of time?
Though we match not the dead men that bore us
  At a song, at a kiss, at a crime--
Though the heathen outface and outlive us,
  And our lives and our longings are twain--
Ah, forgive us our virtues, forgive us,
  Our Lady of Pain.

Who are we that embalm and embrace thee
  With spices and savours of song?
What is time, that his children should face thee?
  What am I, that my lips do thee wrong?
I could hurt thee--but pain would delight thee;
  Or caress thee--but love would repel;
And the lovers whose lips would excite thee
  Are serpents in hell.

Who now shall content thee as they did,
  Thy lovers, when temples were built
And the hair of the sacrifice braided
  And the blood of the sacrifice spilt,
In Lampsacus fervent with faces,
  In Aphaca red from thy reign,
Who embraced thee with awful embraces,
  Our Lady of Pain?

Where are they, Cotytto or Venus,
  Astarte or Ashtaroth, where?
Do their hands as we touch come between us?

Is the breath of them hot in thy hair?
From their lips have thy lips taken fever,
  With the blood of their bodies grown red?
Hast thou left upon earth a believer
  If these men are dead?

They were purple of raiment and golden,
  Filled full of thee, fiery with wine,
Thy lovers, in haunts unbeholden,
  In marvellous chambers of thine.
They are fled, and their footprints escape us,
  Who appraise thee, adore, and abstain,
O daughter of Death and Priapus,
  Our Lady of Pain.

What ails us to fear overmeasure,
  To praise thee with timorous breath,
O mistress and mother of pleasure,
  The one thing as certain as death?
We shall change as the things that we cherish,
  Shall fade as they faded before,
As foam upon water shall perish,
  As sand upon shore.

We shall know what the darkness discovers,
  If the grave-pit be shallow or deep;
And our fathers of old, and our lovers,
  We shall know if they sleep not or sleep.
We shall see whether hell be not heaven,
  Find out whether tares be not grain,
And the joys of thee seventy times seven,
  Our Lady of Pain.

[4] Nam te præcipuè in suis urbibus colit ora
Hellespontia, cæteris ostreosior oris.
CATULL. _Carm._ xviii.

THE GARDEN OF PROSERPINE

Here, where the world is quiet;
  Here, where all trouble seems
Dead winds' and spent waves' riot
  In doubtful dreams of dreams;
I watch the green field growing
  For reaping folk and sowing,
For harvest-time and mowing,
  A sleepy world of streams.

I am tired of tears and laughter,
  And men that laugh and weep;
Of what may come hereafter
  For men that sow to reap:
I am weary of days and hours,
  Blown buds of barren flowers,
Desires and dreams and powers
  And everything but sleep.

Here life has death for neighbour,
  And far from eye or ear
Wan waves and wet winds labour,
  Weak ships and spirits steer;
They drive adrift, and whither
  They wot not who make thither;
But no such winds blow hither,
  And no such things grow here.

No growth of moor or coppice,
  No heather-flower or vine,
But bloomless buds of poppies,
  Green grapes of Proserpine,
Pale beds of blowing rushes
Where no leaf blooms or blushes
Save this whereout she crushes

For dead men deadly wine.

Pale, without name or number,
  In fruitless fields of corn,
They bow themselves and slumber
  All night till light is born;
And like a soul belated,
In hell and heaven unmated,
By cloud and mist abated
  Comes out of darkness morn.

Though one were strong as seven,
  He too with death shall dwell,
Nor wake with wings in heaven,
  Nor weep for pains in hell;
Though one were fair as roses,
His beauty clouds and closes;
And well though love reposes,
  In the end it is not well.

Pale, beyond porch and portal,
  Crowned with calm leaves, she stands
Who gathers all things mortal
  With cold immortal hands;
Her languid lips are sweeter
Than love's who fears to greet her
To men that mix and meet her
  From many times and lands.

She waits for each and other,
  She waits for all men born;
Forgets the earth her mother,
  The life of fruits and corn;
And spring and seed and swallow
Take wing for her and follow
Where summer song rings hollow

And flowers are put to scorn.

There go the loves that wither,
　The old loves with wearier wings;
And all dead years draw thither,
　And all disastrous things;
Dead dreams of days forsaken,
Blind buds that snows have shaken,
Wild leaves that winds have taken,
　Red strays of ruined springs.

We are not sure of sorrow,
　And joy was never sure;
To-day will die to-morrow;
　Time stoops to no man's lure;
And love, grown faint and fretful,
With lips but half regretful
Sighs, and with eyes forgetful
　Weeps that no loves endure.

From too much love of living,
　From hope and fear set free,
We thank with brief thanksgiving
　Whatever gods may be
That no life lives for ever;
That dead men rise up never;
That even the weariest river
　Winds somewhere safe to sea.

Then star nor sun shall waken,
　Nor any change of light:
Nor sound of waters shaken,
　Nor any sound or sight:
Nor wintry leaves nor vernal,
Nor days nor things diurnal;
Only the sleep eternal

In an eternal night.

HESPERIA

Out of the golden remote wild west where the sea without shore is,
    Full of the sunset, and sad, if at all, with the fulness of joy,
As a wind sets in with the autumn that blows from the region of stories,
    Blows with a perfume of songs and of memories beloved from a boy,
Blows from the capes of the past oversea to the bays of the present,
    Filled as with shadow of sound with the pulse of invisible feet,
Far out to the shallows and straits of the future, by rough ways of pleasant,
    Is it thither the wind's wings beat? is it hither to me, O my sweet?
For thee, in the stream of the deep tide-wind blowing in with the water,
    Thee I behold as a bird borne in with the wind from the west,
Straight from the sunset, across white waves whence rose as a daughter
    Venus thy mother, in years when the world was a water at rest.
Out of the distance of dreams, as a dream that abides after slumber,
    Strayed from the fugitive flock of the night, when the moon overhead
Wanes in the wan waste heights of the heaven, and stars without number
    Die without sound, and are spent like lamps that are burnt by the dead,
Comes back to me, stays by me, lulls me with touch of forgotten caresses,

One warm dream clad about with a fire as of life that endures;
The delight of thy face, and the sound of thy feet, and the wind of thy tresses,
And all of a man that regrets, and all of a maid that allures.
But thy bosom is warm for my face and profound as a manifold flower,
Thy silence as music, thy voice as an odour that fades in a flame;
Not a dream, not a dream is the kiss of thy mouth, and the bountiful hour
That makes me forget what was sin, and would make me forget were it shame.
Thine eyes that are quiet, thine hands that are tender, thy lips that are loving,
Comfort and cool me as dew in the dawn of a moon like a dream;
And my heart yearns baffled and blind, moved vainly toward thee, and moving
As the refluent seaweed moves in the languid exuberant stream,
Fair as a rose is on earth, as a rose under water in prison,
That stretches and swings to the slow passionate pulse of the sea,
Closed up from the air and the sun, but alive, as a ghost rearisen,
Pale as the love that revives as a ghost rearisen in me.
From the bountiful infinite west, from the happy memorial places
Full of the stately repose and the lordly delight of the dead,
Where the fortunate islands are lit with the light of ineffable faces,
And the sound of a sea without wind is about them, and sunset is red,

Come back to redeem and release me from love that recalls and represses,
 That cleaves to my flesh as a flame, till the serpent has eaten his fill;
From the bitter delights of the dark, and the feverish, the furtive caresses
 That murder the youth in a man or ever his heart have its will.
Thy lips cannot laugh and thine eyes cannot weep; thou art pale as a rose is,
 Paler and sweeter than leaves that cover the blush of the bud;
And the heart of the flower is compassion, and pity the core it encloses,
 Pity, not love, that is born of the breath and decays with the blood.
As the cross that a wild nun clasps till the edge of it bruises her bosom,
 So love wounds as we grasp it, and blackens and burns as a flame; I have loved overmuch in my life; when the live bud bursts with the blossom,
 Bitter as ashes or tears is the fruit, and the wine thereof shame.
As a heart that its anguish divides is the green bud cloven asunder;
 As the blood of a man self-slain is the flush of the leaves that allure;
And the perfume as poison and wine to the brain, a delight and a wonder;
 And the thorns are too sharp for a boy, too slight for a man, to endure.
Too soon did I love it, and lost love's rose; and I cared not for glory's:
 Only the blossoms of sleep and of pleasure were mixed in my hair.

Was it myrtle or poppy thy garland was woven with, O my Dolores?

Was it pallor of slumber, or blush as of blood, that I found in thee fair?

For desire is a respite from love, and the flesh not the heart is her fuel;

She was sweet to me once, who am fled and escaped from the rage of her reign;

Who behold as of old time at hand as I turn, with her mouth growing cruel,

And flushed as with wine with the blood of her lovers, Our Lady of Pain.

Low down where the thicket is thicker with thorns than with leaves in the summer,

In the brake is a gleaming of eyes and a hissing of tongues that I knew;

And the lithe long throats of her snakes reach round her, their mouths overcome her,

And her lips grow cool with their foam, made moist as a desert with dew.

With the thirst and the hunger of lust though her beautiful lips be so bitter,

With the cold foul foam of the snakes they soften and redden and smile;

And her fierce mouth sweetens, her eyes wax wide and her eyelashes glitter,

And she laughs with a savour of blood in her face, and a savour of guile.

She laughs, and her hands reach hither, her hair blows hither and hisses,

As a low-lit flame in a wind, back-blown till it shudder and leap;

Let her lips not again lay hold on my soul, nor her poisonous kisses,

To consume it alive and divide from thy bosom, Our Lady of Sleep.

Ah daughter of sunset and slumber, if now it return into prison,
 Who shall redeem it anew? but we, if thou wilt, let us fly;
Let us take to us, now that the white skies thrill with a moon unarisen,
 Swift horses of fear or of love, take flight and depart and not die.
They are swifter than dreams, they are stronger than death; there is none that hath ridden,
 None that shall ride in the dim strange ways of his life as we ride;
By the meadows of memory, the highlands of hope, and the shore that is hidden,
 Where life breaks loud and unseen, a sonorous invisible tide;
By the sands where sorrow has trodden, the salt pools bitter and sterile,
 By the thundering reef and the low sea-wall and the channel of years,
Our wild steeds press on the night, strain hard through pleasure and peril,
 Labour and listen and pant not or pause for the peril that nears;
And the sound of them trampling the way cleaves night as an arrow asunder,
 And slow by the sand-hill and swift by the down with its glimpses of grass,
Sudden and steady the music, as eight hoofs trample and thunder,
 Rings in the ear of the low blind wind of the night as we pass;
Shrill shrieks in our faces the blind bland air that was mute as a maiden,
 Stung into storm by the speed of our passage, and deaf where we past;

And our spirits too burn as we bound, thine holy but mine heavy-laden,

As we burn with the fire of our flight; ah love, shall we win at the last?

LOVE AT SEA

We are in love's land to-day;
    Where shall we go?
Love, shall we start or stay,
    Or sail or row?
There's many a wind and way,
And never a May but May;
We are in love's hand to-day;
    Where shall we go?

Our landwind is the breath
Of sorrows kissed to death
    And joys that were;
Our ballast is a rose;
Our way lies where God knows
    And love knows where.
        We are in love's hand to-day--

Our seamen are fledged Loves,
Our masts are bills of doves,
    Our decks fine gold;
Our ropes are dead maids' hair,
Our stores are love-shafts fair
    And manifold.
        We are in love's land to-day--

Where shall we land you, sweet?
On fields of strange men's feet,
    Or fields near home?
Or where the fire-flowers blow,
Or where the flowers of snow
    Or flowers of foam?
        We are in love's hand to-day--

Land me, she says, where love
Shows but one shaft, one dove,
   One heart, one hand.
--A shore like that, my dear,
Lies where no man will steer,
   No maiden land.

Imitated from Théophile Gautier._

APRIL

FROM THE FRENCH OF THE VIDAME DE CHARTRES, 12?? AD

When the fields catch flower
  And the underwood is green,
And from bower unto bower
  The songs of the birds begin,
  I sing with sighing between.
When I laugh and sing,
  I am heavy at heart for my sin;
I am sad in the spring
  For my love that I shall not win,
For a foolish thing.

This profit I have of my woe,
  That I know, as I sing,
I know he will needs have it so
  Who is master and king,
  Who is lord of the spirit of spring.
I will serve her and will not spare
  Till her pity awake
Who is good, who is pure, who is fair,
  Even her for whose sake
Love hath ta'en me and slain unaware.

O my lord, O Love,
  I have laid my life at thy feet;
Have thy will thereof,
  Do as it please thee with it,
  For what shall please thee is sweet.
I am come unto thee
  To do thee service, O Love;
Yet cannot I see

   Thou wilt take any pity thereof,
Any mercy on me.

But the grace I have long time sought
  Comes never in sight,
If in her it abideth not,
  Through thy mercy and might,
  Whose heart is the world's delight.
Thou hast sworn without fail I shall die,
  For my heart is set
On what hurts me, I wot not why,
  But cannot forget
What I love, what I sing for and sigh.

She is worthy of praise,
  For this grief of her giving is worth
All the joy of my days
  That lie between death's day and birth,
  All the lordship of things upon earth.
Nay, what have I said?
  I would not be glad if I could;
My dream and my dread
  Are of her, and for her sake I would
That my life were fled.

Lo, sweet, if I durst not pray to you,
  Then were I dead;
If I sang not a little to say to you,
  (Could it be said)
  O my love, how my heart would be fed;
Ah sweet who hast hold of my heart,
  For thy love's sake I live,
Do but tell me, ere either depart,
  What a lover may give
For a woman so fair as thou art.

The lovers that disbelieve,
  False rumours shall grieve
And evil-speaking shall part.

BEFORE PARTING

A month or twain to live on honeycomb
Is pleasant; but one tires of scented time,
Cold sweet recurrence of accepted rhyme,
And that strong purple under juice and foam
Where the wine's heart has burst;
Nor feel the latter kisses like the first.

Once yet, this poor one time; I will not pray
Even to change the bitterness of it,
The bitter taste ensuing on the sweet,
To make your tears fall where your soft hair lay
All blurred and heavy in some perfumed wise
Over my face and eyes.

And yet who knows what end the scythèd wheat
Makes of its foolish poppies' mouths of red?
These were not sown, these are not harvested,
They grow a month and are cast under feet
And none has care thereof,
As none has care of a divided love.

I know each shadow of your lips by rote,
Each change of love in eyelids and eyebrows;
The fashion of fair temples tremulous
With tender blood, and colour of your throat;
I know not how love is gone out of this,
Seeing that all was his.

Love's likeness there endures upon all these:
But out of these one shall not gather love.
Day hath not strength nor the night shade enough
To make love whole and fill his lips with ease,
As some bee-builded cell
Feels at filled lips the heavy honey swell.

I know not how this last month leaves your hair
Less full of purple colour and hid spice,
And that luxurious trouble of closed eyes
Is mixed with meaner shadow and waste care;
And love, kissed out by pleasure, seems not yet
Worth patience to regret.

THE SUNDEW

A little marsh-plant, yellow green,
And pricked at lip with tender red.
Tread close, and either way you tread
Some faint black water jets between
Lest you should bruise the curious head.

A live thing maybe; who shall know?
The summer knows and suffers it;
For the cool moss is thick and sweet
Each side, and saves the blossom so
That it lives out the long June heat.

The deep scent of the heather burns
About it; breathless though it be,
Bow down and worship; more than we
Is the least flower whose life returns,
Least weed renascent in the sea.

We are vexed and cumbered in earth's sight
With wants, with many memories;
These see their mother what she is,
Glad-growing, till August leave more bright
The apple-coloured cranberries.

Wind blows and bleaches the strong grass,
Blown all one way to shelter it
From trample of strayed kine, with feet
Felt heavier than the moorhen was,
Strayed up past patches of wild wheat.

You call it sundew: how it grows,
If with its colour it have breath,
If life taste sweet to it, if death
Pain its soft petal, no man knows:

Man has no sight or sense that saith.

My sundew, grown of gentle days,
In these green miles the spring begun
Thy growth ere April had half done
With the soft secret of her ways
Or June made ready for the sun.

O red-lipped mouth of marsh-flower,
I have a secret halved with thee.
The name that is love's name to me
Thou knowest, and the face of her
Who is my festival to see.

The hard sun, as thy petals knew,
Coloured the heavy moss-water:
Thou wert not worth green midsummer
Nor fit to live to August blue,
O sundew, not remembering her.

FÉLISE

Mais où sont les neiges d'antan?

What shall be said between us here
  Among the downs, between the trees,
In fields that knew our feet last year,
  In sight of quiet sands and seas,
  This year, Félise?

Who knows what word were best to say?
  For last year's leaves lie dead and red
On this sweet day, in this green May,
  And barren corn makes bitter bread.
  What shall be said?

Here as last year the fields begin,
  A fire of flowers and glowing grass;
The old fields we laughed and lingered in,
  Seeing each our souls in last year's glass,
  Félise, alas!

Shall we not laugh, shall we not weep,
  Not we, though this be as it is?
For love awake or love asleep
  Ends in a laugh, a dream, a kiss,
  A song like this.

I that have slept awake, and you
  Sleep, who last year were well awake,
Though love do all that love can do,
  My heart will never ache or break
  For your heart's sake.

The great sea, faultless as a flower,
  Throbs, trembling under beam and breeze,

And laughs with love of the amorous hour.
  I found you fairer once, Félise,
  Than flowers or seas.

We played at bondsman and at queen;
  But as the days change men change too;
I find the grey sea's notes of green,
  The green sea's fervent flakes of blue,
  More fair than you.

Your beauty is not over fair
  Now in mine eyes, who am grown up wise.
The smell of flowers in all your hair
  Allures not now; no sigh replies
  If your heart sighs.

But you sigh seldom, you sleep sound,
  You find love's new name good enough.
Less sweet I find it than I found
  The sweetest name that ever love
  Grew weary of.

My snake with bright bland eyes, my snake
  Grown tame and glad to be caressed,
With lips athirst for mine to slake
  Their tender fever! who had guessed
  You loved me best?

I had died for this last year, to know
  You loved me. Who shall turn on fate?

I care not if love come or go
  Now, though your love seek mine for mate.
  It is too late.

  The dust of many strange desires

   Lies deep between us; in our eyes
Dead smoke of perishable fires
   Flickers, a fume in air and skies,
   A steam of sighs.

You loved me and you loved me not;
   A little, much, and overmuch.
Will you forget as I forgot?
   Let all dead things lie dead; none such
   Are soft to touch.

I love you and I do not love,
   Too much, a little, not at all;
Too much, and never yet enough.
   Birds quick to fledge and fly at call
   Are quick to fall.

And these love longer now than men,
   And larger loves than ours are these.
No diver brings up love again
   Dropped once, my beautiful Félise,
   In such cold seas.

Gone deeper than all plummets sound,
   Where in the dim green dayless day
The life of such dead things lies bound
   As the sea feeds on, wreck and stray
   And castaway.

Can I forget? yea, that can I,
   And that can all men; so will you,
Alive, or later, when you die.
   Ah, but the love you plead was true?
   Was mine not too?

I loved you for that name of yours

Long ere we met, and long enough.
Now that one thing of all endures--
  The sweetest name that ever love
  Waxed weary of.

Like colours in the sea, like flowers,
  Like a cat's splendid circled eyes
That wax and wane with love for hours,
  Green as green flame, blue-grey like skies,
  And soft like sighs--

And all these only like your name,
  And your name full of all of these.
I say it, and it sounds the same--
  Save that I say it now at ease,
  Your name, Félise.

I said "she must be swift and white,
  And subtly warm, and half perverse,
And sweet like sharp soft fruit to bite,
  And like a snake's love lithe and fierce."
  Men have guessed worse.

What was the song I made of you
  Here where the grass forgets our feet
As afternoon forgets the dew?
  Ah that such sweet things should be fleet,
  Such fleet things sweet!

As afternoon forgets the dew,
  As time in time forgets all men,
As our old place forgets us two,
  Who might have turned to one thing then
  But not again.

    O lips that mine have grown into

    Like April's kissing May,
    O fervent eyelids letting through
    Those eyes the greenest of things blue,
      The bluest of things grey,

    If you were I and I were you,
      How could I love you, say?
    How could the roseleaf love the rue,
    The day love nightfall and her dew,
      Though night may love the day?

You loved it may be more than I;
  We know not; love is hard to seize.
And all things are not good to try;
  And lifelong loves the worst of these
  For us, Félise.

Ah, take the season and have done,
  Love well the hour and let it go:
Two souls may sleep and wake up one,
  Or dream they wake and find it so,
  And then--you know.

Kiss me once hard as though a flame
  Lay on my lips and made them fire;

The same lips now, and not the same;
  What breath shall fill and re-inspire
  A dead desire?

The old song sounds hollower in mine ear
  Than thin keen sounds of dead men's speech--
A noise one hears and would not hear;
  Too strong to die, too weak to reach
  From wave to beach.

We stand on either side the sea,
  Stretch hands, blow kisses, laugh and lean
I toward you, you toward me;
  But what hears either save the keen
  Grey sea between?

A year divides us, love from love,
  Though you love now, though I loved then.
The gulf is strait, but deep enough;
  Who shall recross, who among men
  Shall cross again?

Love was a jest last year, you said,
  And what lives surely, surely dies.
Even so; but now that love is dead,
  Shall love rekindle from wet eyes,
  From subtle sighs?

For many loves are good to see;
  Mutable loves, and loves perverse;
But there is nothing, nor shall be,
  So sweet, so wicked, but my verse
  Can dream of worse.

For we that sing and you that love
  Know that which man may, only we.
The rest live under us; above,
  Live the great gods in heaven, and see
  What things shall be.

So this thing is and must be so;
  For man dies, and love also dies.
Though yet love's ghost moves to and fro
  The sea-green mirrors of your eyes,
  And laughs, and lies.

Eyes coloured like a water-flower,
  And deeper than the green sea's glass;
Eyes that remember one sweet hour--
  In vain we swore it should not pass;
  In vain, alas!

Ah my Félise, if love or sin,
  If shame or fear could hold it fast,
Should we not hold it? Love wears thin,
  And they laugh well who laugh the last.
  Is it not past?

The gods, the gods are stronger; time
  Falls down before them, all men's knees
Bow, all men's prayers and sorrows climb
  Like incense towards them; yea, for these
  Are gods, Félise.

Immortal are they, clothed with powers,
  Not to be comforted at all;
Lords over all the fruitless hours;
  Too great to appease, too high to appal,
  Too far to call.
For none shall move the most high gods,
  Who are most sad, being cruel; none
Shall break or take away the rods
  Wherewith they scourge us, not as one
  That smites a son.

By many a name of many a creed
  We have called upon them, since the sands
Fell through time's hour-glass first, a seed
  Of life; and out of many lands
  Have we stretched hands.

When have they heard us? who hath known
  Their faces, climbed unto their feet,
Felt them and found them? Laugh or groan,
  Doth heaven remurmur and repeat
   Sad sounds or sweet?

Do the stars answer? in the night
  Have ye found comfort? or by day
Have ye seen gods? What hope, what light,
  Falls from the farthest starriest way
   On you that pray?

Are the skies wet because we weep,
  Or fair because of any mirth?
Cry out; they are gods; perchance they sleep;
  Cry; thou shalt know what prayers are worth,
   Thou dust and earth.

O earth, thou art fair; O dust, thou art great;
  O laughing lips and lips that mourn,
Pray, till ye feel the exceeding weight
  Of God's intolerable scorn,
   Not to be borne.
Behold, there is no grief like this;
  The barren blossom of thy prayer,
Thou shalt find out how sweet it is.
  O fools and blind, what seek ye there,
   High up in the air?

Ye must have gods, the friends of men,
  Merciful gods, compassionate,
And these shall answer you again.
  Will ye beat always at the gate,
   Ye fools of fate?

Ye fools and blind; for this is sure,

That all ye shall not live, but die.
Lo, what thing have ye found endure?
  Or what thing have ye found on high
  Past the blind sky?

The ghosts of words and dusty dreams,
  Old memories, faiths infirm and dead.
Ye fools; for which among you deems
  His prayer can alter green to red
  Or stones to bread?

Why should ye bear with hopes and fears
  Till all these things be drawn in one,
The sound of iron-footed years,
  And all the oppression that is done
  Under the sun?

Ye might end surely, surely pass
  Out of the multitude of things,
Under the dust, beneath the grass,

Deep in dim death, where no thought stings,
  No record clings.

No memory more of love or hate,
  No trouble, nothing that aspires,
No sleepless labour thwarting fate,
  And thwarted; where no travail tires,
  Where no faith fires.

All passes, nought that has been is,
  Things good and evil have one end.
Can anything be otherwise
  Though all men swear all things would mend
  With God to friend?

Can ye beat off one wave with prayer,
  Can ye move mountains? bid the flower
Take flight and turn to a bird in the air?
  Can ye hold fast for shine or shower
  One wingless hour?

Ah sweet, and we too, can we bring
  One sigh back, bid one smile revive?
Can God restore one ruined thing,
  Or he who slays our souls alive
  Make dead things thrive?

Two gifts perforce he has given us yet,
  Though sad things stay and glad things fly;
Two gifts he has given us, to forget
  All glad and sad things that go by,
  And then to die.

We know not whether death be good,
  But life at least it will not be:
Men will stand saddening as we stood,
  Watch the same fields and skies as we
  And the same sea.

Let this be said between us here,
  One love grows green when one turns grey;
This year knows nothing of last year;
  To-morrow has no more to say
  To yesterday.

Live and let live, as I will do,
  Love and let love, and so will I.
But, sweet, for me no more with you:
  Not while I live, not though I die.
  Goodnight, goodbye.

AN INTERLUDE

In the greenest growth of the Maytime,
  I rode where the woods were wet,
Between the dawn and the daytime;
  The spring was glad that we met.

There was something the season wanted,
  Though the ways and the woods smelt sweet;
The breath at your lips that panted,
The pulse of the grass at your feet.

You came, and the sun came after,
  And the green grew golden above;
And the flag-flowers lightened with laughter,
  And the meadow-sweet shook with love.

Your feet in the full-grown grasses
  Moved soft as a weak wind blows;
You passed me as April passes,
  With face made out of a rose.

By the stream where the stems were slender,
  Your bright foot paused at the sedge;
It might be to watch the tender
  Light leaves in the springtime hedge,

On boughs that the sweet month blanches
  With flowery frost of May:
It might be a bird in the branches,
  It might be a thorn in the way.

I waited to watch you linger
  With foot drawn back from the dew,
Till a sunbeam straight like a finger
  Struck sharp through the leaves at you.

And a bird overhead sang _Follow_,
  And a bird to the right sang _Here_;
And the arch of the leaves was hollow,
  And the meaning of May was clear.

I saw where the sun's hand pointed,
  I knew what the bird's note said;
By the dawn and the dewfall anointed,
  You were queen by the gold on your head.

As the glimpse of a burnt-out ember
  Recalls a regret of the sun,
I remember, forget, and remember
  What Love saw done and undone.

I remember the way we parted,
  The day and the way we met;
You hoped we were both broken-hearted,
  And knew we should both forget.

And May with her world in flower
  Seemed still to murmur and smile
As you murmured and smiled for an hour;
  I saw you turn at the stile.

A hand like a white wood-blossom
  You lifted, and waved, and passed,
With head hung down to the bosom,
  And pale, as it seemed, at last.

And the best and the worst of this is
  That neither is most to blame
If you've forgotten my kisses
  And I've forgotten your name.

HENDECASYLLABICS

In the month of the long decline of roses
I, beholding the summer dead before me,
Set my face to the sea and journeyed silent,
Gazing eagerly where above the sea-mark
Flame as fierce as the fervid eyes of lions
Half divided the eyelids of the sunset;
Till I heard as it were a noise of waters
Moving tremulous under feet of angels
Multitudinous, out of all the heavens;
Knew the fluttering wind, the fluttered foliage,
Shaken fitfully, full of sound and shadow;
And saw, trodden upon by noiseless angels,
Long mysterious reaches fed with moonlight,
Sweet sad straits in a soft subsiding channel,
Blown about by the lips of winds I knew not,
Winds not born in the north nor any quarter,
Winds not warm with the south nor any sunshine;
Heard between them a voice of exultation,
"Lo, the summer is dead, the sun is faded,
Even like as a leaf the year is withered,
All the fruits of the day from all her branches
Gathered, neither is any left to gather.
All the flowers are dead, the tender blossoms,
All are taken away; the season wasted,
Like an ember among the fallen ashes.
Now with light of the winter days, with moonlight,
Light of snow, and the bitter light of hoarfrost,
We bring flowers that fade not after autumn,
Pale white chaplets and crowns of latter seasons,
Fair false leaves (but the summer leaves were falser),
Woven under the eyes of stars and planets
When low light was upon the windy reaches
Where the flower of foam was blown, a lily
Dropt among the sonorous fruitless furrows

And green fields of the sea that make no pasture:
Since the winter begins, the weeping winter,
All whose flowers are tears, and round his temples
Iron blossom of frost is bound for ever."

SAPPHICS

All the night sleep came not upon my eyelids,
Shed not dew, nor shook nor unclosed a feather,
Yet with lips shut close and with eyes of iron
  Stood and beheld me.

Then to me so lying awake a vision
Came without sleep over the seas and touched me,
Softly touched mine eyelids and lips; and I too,
  Full of the vision,

Saw the white implacable Aphrodite,
Saw the hair unbound and the feet unsandalled
Shine as fire of sunset on western waters;
  Saw the reluctant

Feet, the straining plumes of the doves that drew her,
Looking always, looking with necks reverted,
Back to Lesbos, back to the hills whereunder
  Shone Mitylene;

Heard the flying feet of the Loves behind her
Make a sudden thunder upon the waters,
As the thunder flung from the strong unclosing
  Wings of a great wind.

So the goddess fled from her place, with awful
Sound of feet and thunder of wings around her;
While behind a clamour of singing women
  Severed the twilight.

Ah the singing, ah the delight, the passion!
  All the Loves wept, listening; sick with anguish,
  Stood the crowned nine Muses about Apollo;

Fear was upon them,

While the tenth sang wonderful things they knew not.
Ah the tenth, the Lesbian! the nine were silent,
None endured the sound of her song for weeping;
  Laurel by laurel,

Faded all their crowns; but about her forehead,
Round her woven tresses and ashen temples
White as dead snow, paler than grass in summer,
  Ravaged with kisses,

Shone a light of fire as a crown for ever.
Yea, almost the implacable Aphrodite
Paused, and almost wept; such a song was that song.
  Yea, by her name too

Called her, saying, "Turn to me, O my Sappho;"
Yet she turned her face from the Loves, she saw not
Tears for laughter darken immortal eyelids,
  Heard not about her

Fearful fitful wings of the doves departing,
Saw not how the bosom of Aphrodite
Shook with weeping, saw not her shaken raiment,
  Saw not her hands wrung;

Saw the Lesbians kissing across their smitten
Lutes with lips more sweet than the sound of lute-strings,
Mouth to mouth and hand upon hand, her chosen,
  Fairer than all men;

Only saw the beautiful lips and fingers,
Full of songs and kisses and little whispers,
Full of music; only beheld among them
  Soar, as a bird soars

Newly fledged, her visible song, a marvel,
Made of perfect sound and exceeding passion,
Sweetly shapen, terrible, full of thunders,
  Clothed with the wind's wings.

Then rejoiced she, laughing with love, and scattered
Roses, awful roses of holy blossom;
Then the Loves thronged sadly with hidden faces
  Round Aphrodite,

Then the Muses, stricken at heart, were silent;
Yea, the gods waxed pale; such a song was that song.
All reluctant, all with a fresh repulsion,
  Fled from before her.

All withdrew long since, and the land was barren,
Full of fruitless women and music only.
Now perchance, when winds are assuaged at sunset,
  Lulled at the dewfall,

By the grey sea-side, unassuaged, unheard of,
Unbeloved, unseen in the ebb of twilight,
Ghosts of outcast women return lamenting,
  Purged not in Lethe,

Clothed about with flame and with tears, and singing
Songs that move the heart of the shaken heaven,
Songs that break the heart of the earth with pity,
  Hearing, to hear them.

AT ELEUSIS

Men of Eleusis, ye that with long staves
Sit in the market-houses, and speak words
Made sweet with wisdom as the rare wine is
Thickened with honey; and ye sons of these
Who in the glad thick streets go up and down
For pastime or grave traffic or mere chance;
And all fair women having rings of gold
On hands or hair; and chiefest over these
I name you, daughters of this man the king,
Who dipping deep smooth pitchers of pure brass
Under the bubbled wells, till each round lip
Stooped with loose gurgle of waters incoming,
Found me an old sick woman, lamed and lean,
Beside a growth of builded olive-boughs
Whence multiplied thick song of thick-plumed throats--
Also wet tears filled up my hollow hands
By reason of my crying into them--
And pitied me; for as cold water ran
And washed the pitchers full from lip to lip,
So washed both eyes full the strong salt of tears.
And ye put water to my mouth, made sweet
With brown hill-berries; so in time I spoke
And gathered my loose knees from under me.
Moreover in the broad fair halls this month
Have I found space and bountiful abode
To please me. I Demeter speak of this,
Who am the mother and the mate of things:
For as ill men by drugs or singing words
Shut the doors inward of the narrowed womb
Like a lock bolted with round iron through,
Thus I shut up the body and sweet mouth
Of all soft pasture and the tender land,
So that no seed can enter in by it
Though one sow thickly, nor some grain get out

Past the hard clods men cleave and bite with steel
To widen the sealed lips of them for use.
None of you is there in the peopled street
But knows how all the dry-drawn furrows ache
With no green spot made count of in the black:
How the wind finds no comfortable grass
Nor is assuaged with bud nor breath of herbs;
And in hot autumn when ye house the stacks,
All fields are helpless in the sun, all trees
Stand as a man stripped out of all but skin.
Nevertheless ye sick have help to get
By means and stablished ordinance of God;
For God is wiser than a good man is.
But never shall new grass be sweet in earth
Till I get righted of my wound and wrong
By changing counsel of ill-minded Zeus.
For of all other gods is none save me
Clothed with like power to build and break the year.
I make the lesser green begin, when spring
Touches not earth but with one fearful foot;
And as a careful gilder with grave art
Soberly colours and completes the face,
Mouth, chin and all, of some sweet work in stone,
I carve the shapes of grass and tender corn
And colour the ripe edges and long spikes
With the red increase and the grace of gold,
No tradesman in soft wools is cunninger
To kill the secret of the fat white fleece
With stains of blue and purple wrought in it.
Three moons were made and three moons burnt away
While I held journey hither out of Crete
Comfortless, tended by grave Hecate
Whom my wound stung with double iron point;
For all my face was like a cloth wrung out
With close and weeping wrinkles, and both lids
Sodden with salt continuance of tears.

For Hades and the sidelong will of Zeus
And that lame wisdom that has writhen feet,
Cunning, begotten in the bed of Shame,
These three took evil will at me, and made
Such counsel that when time got wing to fly
This Hades out of summer and low fields
Forced the bright body of Persephone:
Out of pure grass, where she lying down, red flowers
Made their sharp little shadows on her sides,
Pale heat, pale colour on pale maiden flesh--
And chill water slid over her reddening feet,
Killing the throbs in their soft blood; and birds,
Perched next her elbow and pecking at her hair,
Stretched their necks more to see her than even to sing.
A sharp thing is it I have need to say;
For Hades holding both white wrists of hers
Unloosed the girdle and with knot by knot
Bound her between his wheels upon the seat,
Bound her pure body, holiest yet and dear
To me and God as always, clothed about
With blossoms loosened as her knees went down.
Let fall as she let go of this and this
By tens and twenties, tumbled to her feet,
White waifs or purple of the pasturage.
Therefore with only going up and down
My feet were wasted, and the gracious air,
To me discomfortable and dun, became
As weak smoke blowing in the under world.
And finding in the process of ill days
What part had Zeus herein, and how as mate
He coped with Hades, yokefellow in sin,
I set my lips against the meat of gods
And drank not neither ate or slept in heaven.
Nor in the golden greeting of their mouths
Did ear take note of me, nor eye at all
Track my feet going in the ways of them.

Like a great fire on some strait slip of land
Between two washing inlets of wet sea
That burns the grass up to each lip of beach
And strengthens, waxing in the growth of wind,
So burnt my soul in me at heaven and earth,
Each way a ruin and a hungry plague,
Visible evil; nor could any night
Put cool between mine eyelids, nor the sun
With competence of gold fill out my want.
Yea so my flame burnt up the grass and stones,
Shone to the salt-white edges of thin sea,
Distempered all the gracious work, and made
Sick change, unseasonable increase of days
And scant avail of seasons; for by this
The fair gods faint in hollow heaven: there comes
No taste of burnings of the twofold fat
To leave their palates smooth, nor in their lips
Soft rings of smoke and weak scent wandering;
All cattle waste and rot, and their ill smell
Grows alway from the lank unsavoury flesh
That no man slays for offering; the sea
And waters moved beneath the heath and corn
Preserve the people of fin-twinkling fish,
And river-flies feed thick upon the smooth;
But all earth over is no man or bird
(Except the sweet race of the kingfisher)
That lacks not and is wearied with much loss.
Meantime the purple inward of the house
Was softened with all grace of scent and sound
In ear and nostril perfecting my praise;
Faint grape-flowers and cloven honey-cake
And the just grain with dues of the shed salt
Made me content: yet my hand loosened not
Its gripe upon your harvest all year long.
While I, thus woman-muffled in wan flesh
And waste externals of a perished face,

Preserved the levels of my wrath and love
Patiently ruled; and with soft offices
Cooled the sharp noons and busied the warm nights
In care of this my choice, this child my choice,
Triptolemus, the king's selected son:
That this fair yearlong body, which hath grown
Strong with strange milk upon the mortal lip
And nerved with half a god, might so increase
Outside the bulk and the bare scope of man:
And waxen over large to hold within
Base breath of yours and this impoverished air,
I might exalt him past the flame of stars,
The limit and walled reach of the great world.
Therefore my breast made common to his mouth
Immortal savours, and the taste whereat
Twice their hard life strains out the coloured veins
And twice its brain confirms the narrow shell.
Also at night, unwinding cloth from cloth
As who unhusks an almond to the white
And pastures curiously the purer taste,
I bared the gracious limbs and the soft feet,
Unswaddled the weak hands, and in mid ash
Laid the sweet flesh of either feeble side,
More tender for impressure of some touch
Than wax to any pen; and lit around
Fire, and made crawl the white worm-shapen flame,
And leap in little angers spark by spark
At head at once and feet; and the faint hair
Hissed with rare sprinkles in the closer curl,
And like scaled oarage of a keen thin fish
In sea-water, so in pure fire his feet
Struck out, and the flame bit not in his flesh,
But like a kiss it curled his lip, and heat
Fluttered his eyelids; so each night I blew
The hot ash red to purge him to full god.
Ill is it when fear hungers in the soul

For painful food, and chokes thereon, being fed;
And ill slant eyes interpret the straight sun,
But in their scope its white is wried to black:
By the queen Metaneira mean I this;
For with sick wrath upon her lips, and heart
Narrowing with fear the spleenful passages,
She thought to thread this web's fine ravel out,
Nor leave her shuttle split in combing it;
Therefore she stole on us, and with hard sight
Peered, and stooped close; then with pale open mouth
As the fire smote her in the eyes between
Cried, and the child's laugh, sharply shortening
As fire doth under rain, fell off; the flame
Writhed once all through and died, and in thick dark
Tears fell from mine on the child's weeping eyes,
Eyes dispossessed of strong inheritance
And mortal fallen anew. Who not the less
From bud of beard to pale-grey flower of hair
Shall wax vinewise to a lordly vine, whose grapes
Bleed the red heavy blood of swoln soft wine,
Subtle with sharp leaves' intricacy, until
Full of white years and blossom of hoary days
I take him perfected; for whose one sake
I am thus gracious to the least who stands
Filleted with white wool and girt upon
As he whose prayer endures upon the lip
And falls not waste: wherefore let sacrifice
Burn and run red in all the wider ways;
Seeing I have sworn by the pale temples' band
And poppied hair of gold Persephone
Sad-tressed and pleached low down about her brows,
And by the sorrow in her lips, and death
Her dumb and mournful-mouthèd minister,
My word for you is eased of its harsh weight
And doubled with soft promise; and your king
Triptolemus, this Celeus dead and swathed

Purple and pale for golden burial,
Shall be your helper in my services,
Dividing earth and reaping fruits thereof
In fields where wait, well-girt, well-wreathen, all
The heavy-handed seasons all year through;
Saving the choice of warm spear-headed grain,
And stooping sharp to the slant-sided share
All beasts that furrow the remeasured land
With their bowed necks of burden equable.

AUGUST

There were four apples on the bough,
Half gold half red, that one might know
The blood was ripe inside the core;
The colour of the leaves was more
Like stems of yellow corn that grow
Through all the gold June meadow's floor.

The warm smell of the fruit was good
To feed on, and the split green wood,
With all its bearded lips and stains
Of mosses in the cloven veins,
Most pleasant, if one lay or stood
In sunshine or in happy rains.

There were four apples on the tree,
Red stained through gold, that all might see
The sun went warm from core to rind;
The green leaves made the summer blind
In that soft place they kept for me
With golden apples shut behind.

The leaves caught gold across the sun,
And where the bluest air begun
Thirsted for song to help the heat;
As I to feel my lady's feet
Draw close before the day were done;
Both lips grew dry with dreams of it.

In the mute August afternoon
They trembled to some undertune
Of music in the silver air;
Great pleasure was it to be there
Till green turned duskier and the moon
Coloured the corn-sheaves like gold hair.

That August time it was delight
To watch the red moons wane to white
'Twixt grey seamed stems of apple-trees;
A sense of heavy harmonies
Grew on the growth of patient night,
More sweet than shapen music is.

But some three hours before the moon
The air, still eager from the noon,
Flagged after heat, not wholly dead;
Against the stem I leant my head;
The colour soothed me like a tune,
Green leaves all round the gold and red.

I lay there till the warm smell grew
More sharp, when flecks of yellow dew
Between the round ripe leaves had blurred
The rind with stain and wet; I heard
A wind that blew and breathed and blew,
Too weak to alter its one word.

The wet leaves next the gentle fruit
Felt smoother, and the brown tree-root
Felt the mould warmer: I too felt
(As water feels the slow gold melt
Right through it when the day burns mute)
The peace of time wherein love dwelt.

There were four apples on the tree,
Gold stained on red that all might see
The sweet blood filled them to the core:
The colour of her hair is more
Like stems of fair faint gold, that be
Mown from the harvest's middle floor.

A CHRISTMAS CAROL

Suggested by a drawing of Mr. D. G. Rossetti's.

Three damsels in the queen's chamber,
   The queen's mouth was most fair;
She spake a word of God's mother
   As the combs went in her hair.
     Mary that is of might,
     Bring us to thy Son's sight.

They held the gold combs out from her,
   A span's length off her head;
She sang this song of God's mother
   And of her bearing-bed.
     Mary most full of grace,
     Bring us to thy Son's face.

When she sat at Joseph's hand,
   She looked against her side;
And either way from the short silk band
   Her girdle was all wried.
     Mary that all good may,
     Bring us to thy Son's way.

Mary had three women for her bed,
   The twain were maidens clean;
The first of them had white and red,
   The third had riven green.
     Mary that is so sweet,
     Bring us to thy Son's feet.

She had three women for her hair,
   Two were gloved soft and shod;
The third had feet and fingers bare,
   She was the likest God.

Mary that wieldeth land,
Bring us to thy Son's hand.

She had three women for her ease,
  The twain were good women:
The first two were the two Maries,
  The third was Magdalen.
    Mary that perfect is,
    Bring us to thy Son's kiss.

Joseph had three workmen in his stall,
  To serve him well upon;
The first of them were Peter and Paul,
  The third of them was John.
    Mary, God's handmaiden,
    Bring us to thy Son's ken.

"If your child be none other man's,
  But if it be very mine,
The bedstead shall be gold two spans,
  The bedfoot silver fine."
    Mary that made God mirth,
    Bring us to thy Son's birth.

"If the child be some other man's,
  And if it be none of mine,
The manger shall be straw two spans,
  Betwixen kine and kine."
    Mary that made sin cease,
    Bring us to thy Son's peace.

Christ was born upon this wise,
  It fell on such a night,
Neither with sounds of psalteries,
  Nor with fire for light.
    Mary that is God's spouse,

  Bring us to thy Son's house.

The star came out upon the east
  With a great sound and sweet:
Kings gave gold to make him feast
  And myrrh for him to eat.
   Mary, of thy sweet mood,
   Bring us to thy Son's good.

He had two handmaids at his head,
  One handmaid at his feet;
The twain of them were fair and red,
  The third one was right sweet.
   Mary that is most wise,
   Bring us to thy Son's eyes. Amen.

THE MASQUE OF QUEEN BERSABE

A MIRACLE-PLAY

KING DAVID

Knights mine, all that be in hall,
I have a counsel to you all,
Because of this thing God lets fall
    Among us for a sign.
For some days hence as I did eat
From kingly dishes my good meat,
There flew a bird between my feet
    As red as any wine.
This bird had a long bill of red
And a gold ring above his head;
Long time he sat and nothing said,
Put softly down his neck and fed
    From the gilt patens fine:
And as I marvelled, at the last
He shut his two keen eyën fast
And suddenly woxe big and brast
    Ere one should tell to nine.

PRIMUS MILES

Sir, note this that I will say;
That Lord who maketh corn with hay
And morrows each of yesterday,
    He hath you in his hand,

SECUNDUS MILES (_Paganus quidam_)

By Satan I hold no such thing;
For if wine swell within a king
Whose ears for drink are hot and ring,
The same shall dream of wine-bibbing
   Whilst he can lie or stand.

QUEEN BERSABE

Peace now, lords, for Godis head,
Ye chirk as starlings that be fed
And gape as fishes newly dead;
The devil put your bones to bed,
   Lo, this is all to say.

SECUNDUS MILES

By Mahound, lords, I have good will
This devil's bird to wring and spill;
For now meseems our game goes ill,
   Ye have scant hearts to play.

TERTIUS MILES

Lo, sirs, this word is there said,
That Urias the knight is dead
Through some ill craft; by Poulis head,
I doubt his blood hath made so red
This bird that flew from the queen's bed
   Whereof ye have such fear.

KING DAVID

Yea, my good knave, and is it said
That I can raise men from the dead?
By God I think to have his head
Who saith words of my lady's bed
   For any thief to hear.
   Et percutiat eum in capite.

QUEEN BERSABE

I wis men shall spit at me,
And say, it were but right for thee
That one should hang thee on a tree;
Ho! it were a fair thing to see
The big stones bruise her false body;
   Fie! who shall see her dead?

KING DAVID

I rede you have no fear of this,
For, as ye wot, the first good kiss
I had must be the last of his;
Now are ye queen of mine, I wis,
And lady of a house that is
   Full rich of meat and bread.

PRIMUS MILES

I bid you make good cheer to be
So fair a queen as all men see.
And hold us for your lieges free;
By Peter's soul that hath the key,
   Ye have good hap of it.

SECUNDUS MILES

I would that he were hanged and dead
Who hath no joy to see your head
With gold about it, barred on red;
I hold him as a sow of lead
    That is so scant of wit.

Tunc dicat NATHAN propheta_

O king, I have a word to thee;
The child that is in Bersabe
Shall wither without light to see;
This word is come of God by me
    For sin that ye have done.
Because herein ye did not right,
To take the fair one lamb to smite
That was of Urias the knight;
    Ye wist he had but one.
Full many sheep I wot ye had,
And many women, when ye bade,
To do your will and keep you glad,
And a good crown about your head
    With gold to show thereon.
This Urias had one poor house
With low-barred latoun shot-windows
And scant of corn to fill a mouse;
And rusty basnets for his brows,
    To wear them to the bone.
Yea the roofs also, as men sain,
Were thin to hold against the rain;
Therefore what rushes were there lain
Grew wet withouten foot of men;
The stancheons were all gone in twain

   As sick man's flesh is gone.
Nathless he had great joy to see
The long hair of this Bersabe
Fall round her lap and round her knee
Even to her small soft feet, that be
Shod now with crimson royally
   And covered with clean gold.
Likewise great joy he had to kiss
Her throat, where now the scarlet is
Against her little chin, I wis,
   That then was but cold.
No scarlet then her kirtle had
And little gold about it sprad;
But her red mouth was always glad
To kiss, albeit the eyes were sad
   With love they had to hold.

SECUNDUS MILES

How! old thief, thy wits are lame;
To clip such it is no shame;
I rede you in the devil's name,
Ye come not here to make men game;
By Termagaunt that maketh grame,
   I shall to-bete thine head.
   Hìc Diabolus capiat eum.
This knave hath sharp fingers, perfay;
Mahound you thank and keep alway,
And give you good knees to pray;
What man hath no lust to play,
The devil wring his ears, I say;
There is no more but wellaway,
   For now am I dead.

KING DAVID

Certes his mouth is wried and black,
Full little pence be in his sack;
This devil hath him by the back,
   It is no boot to lie.

NATHAN

Sitteth now still and learn of me;
A little while and ye shall see
The face of God's strength presently.
All queens made as this Bersabe,
All that were fair and foul ye be,
   Come hither; it am I.

  Et hìc omnes cantabunt.

HERODIAS

I am the queen Herodias.
This headband of my temples was
   King Herod's gold band woven me.
This broken dry staff in my hand
Was the queen's staff of a great land
   Betwixen Perse and Samarie.
For that one dancing of my feet,
The fire is come in my green wheat,
   From one sea to the other sea.

AHOLIBAH

I am the queen Aholibah.

My lips kissed dumb the word of _Ah_
   Sighed on strange lips grown sick thereby.
God wrought to me my royal bed;
The inner work thereof was red,
   The outer work was ivory.
My mouth's heat was the heat of flame
For lust towards the kings that came
   With horsemen riding royally.

CLEOPATRA

I am the queen of Ethiope.
Love bade my kissing eyelids ope
   That men beholding might praise love.
My hair was wonderful and curled;
My lips held fast the mouth o' the world
   To spoil the strength and speech thereof.
The latter triumph in my breath
Bowed down the beaten brows of death,
   Ashamed they had not wrath enough.

ABIHAIL

I am the queen of Tyrians.
My hair was glorious for twelve spans,
   That dried to loose dust afterward.
My stature was a strong man's length:
My neck was like a place of strength
   Built with white walls, even and hard,
Like the first noise of rain leaves catch
One from another, snatch by snatch,
   Is my praise, hissed against and marred.

AZUBAH

I am the queen of Amorites.
My face was like a place of lights
   With multitudes at festival.
The glory of my gracious brows
Was like God's house made glorious
   With colours upon either wall.
Between my brows and hair there was
A white space like a space of glass
   With golden candles over all.

AHOLAH

I am the queen of Amalek.
There was no tender touch or fleck
   To spoil my body or bared feet.
My words were soft like dulcimers,
And the first sweet of grape-flowers
   Made each side of my bosom sweet.
My raiment was as tender fruit
Whose rind smells sweet of spice-tree root,
   Bruised balm-blossom and budded wheat.

AHINOAM

I am the queen Ahinoam.
Like the throat of a soft slain lamb
   Was my throat, softer veined than his:
My lips were as two grapes the sun
Lays his whole weight of heat upon
   Like a mouth heavy with a kiss:
My hair's pure purple a wrought fleece,

My temples therein as a piece
    Of a pomegranate's cleaving is.

ATARAH

I am the queen Sidonian.
My face made faint the face of man,
    And strength was bound between my brows
Spikenard was hidden in my ships,
Honey and wheat and myrrh in strips,
    White wools that shine as colour does,
Soft linen dyed upon the fold,
Split spice and cores of scented gold,
    Cedar and broken calamus.

SEMIRAMIS

I am the queen Semiramis.
The whole world and the sea that is
    In fashion like a chrysopras,
The noise of all men labouring,
The priest's mouth tired through thanksgiving,
    The sound of love in the blood's pause,
The strength of love in the blood's beat,
All these were cast beneath my feet
    And all found lesser than I was.

HESIONE

I am the queen Hesione.
The seasons that increased in me
    Made my face fairer than all men's.
I had the summer in my hair;

And all the pale gold autumn air
   Was as the habit of my sense.
My body was as fire that shone;
God's beauty that makes all things one
   Was one among my handmaidens.

CHRYSOTHEMIS

I am the queen of Samothrace.
God, making roses, made my face
   As a rose filled up full with red.
My prows made sharp the straitened seas
From Pontus to that Chersonese
   Whereon the ebbed Asian stream is shed.
My hair was as sweet scent that drips;
Love's breath begun about my lips
   Kindled the lips of people dead.

THOMYRIS

I am the queen of Scythians.
My strength was like no strength of man's,
   My face like day, my breast like spring.
My fame was felt in the extreme land
That hath sunshine on the one hand
   And on the other star-shining.
Yea, and the wind there fails of breath;
Yea, and there life is waste like death;
   Yea, and there death is a glad thing.

HARHAS

I am the queen of Anakim.

In the spent years whose speech is dim,
    Whose raiment is the dust and death,
My stately body without stain
Shone as the shining race of rain
    Whose hair a great wind scattereth.
Now hath God turned my lips to sighs,
Plucked off mine eyelids from mine eyes,
    And sealed with seals my way of breath.

MYRRHA

I am the queen Arabian.
The tears wherewith mine eyelids ran
    Smelt like my perfumed eyelids' smell.
A harsh thirst made my soft mouth hard,
That ached with kisses afterward;
    My brain rang like a beaten bell.
As tears on eyes, as fire on wood,
Sin fed upon my breath and blood,
    Sin made my breasts subside and swell.

PASIPHAE

I am the queen Pasiphae.
Not all the pure clean-coloured sea
    Could cleanse or cool my yearning veins;
Nor any root nor herb that grew,
Flag-leaves that let green water through,
    Nor washing of the dews and rains.
From shame's pressed core I wrung the sweet
Fruit's savour that was death to eat,
    Whereof no seed but death remains.

SAPPHO

I am the queen of Lesbians.
My love, that had no part in man's,
   Was sweeter than all shape of sweet.
The intolerable infinite desire
Made my face pale like faded fire
   When the ashen pyre falls through with heat.
My blood was hot wan wine of love,
And my song's sound the sound thereof,
   The sound of the delight of it.

MESSALINA

I am the queen of Italy.
These were the signs God set on me;
   A barren beauty subtle and sleek,
Curled carven hair, and cheeks worn wan
With fierce false lips of many a man,
   Large temples where the blood ran weak,
A mouth athirst and amorous

And hungering as the grave's mouth does
   That, being an-hungred, cannot speak.

AMESTRIS

I am the queen of Persians.
My breasts were lordlier than bright swans.
   My body as amber fair and thin.
Strange flesh was given my lips for bread,
With poisonous hours my days were fed,
   And my feet shod with adder-skin.
In Shushan toward Ecbatane

I wrought my joys with tears and pain,
   My loves with blood and bitter sin.

EPHRATH

I am the queen of Rephaim.
God, that some while refraineth him,
   Made in the end a spoil of me.
My rumour was upon the world
As strong sound of swoln water hurled
   Through porches of the straining sea.
My hair was like the flag-flower,
And my breasts carven goodlier
   Than beryl with chalcedony.

PASITHEA

I am the queen of Cypriotes.
Mine oarsmen, labouring with brown throats,
   Sang of me many a tender thing.
My maidens, girdled loose and braced
With gold from bosom to white waist,
   Praised me between their wool-combing.
All that praise Venus all night long
With lips like speech and lids like song
   Praised me till song lost heart to sing.

ALACIEL

I am the queen Alaciel.
My mouth was like that moist gold cell
   Whereout the thickest honey drips.
Mine eyes were as a grey-green sea;

The amorous blood that smote on me
    Smote to my feet and finger-tips.
My throat was whiter than the dove,
Mine eyelids as the seals of love,
    And as the doors of love my lips.

ERIGONE

I am the queen Erigone.
The wild wine shed as blood on me
    Made my face brighter than a bride's.
My large lips had the old thirst of earth,
Mine arms the might of the old sea's girth
    Bound round the whole world's iron sides.
Within mine eyes and in mine ears
Were music and the wine of tears,
    And light, and thunder of the tides.
    Et hìc exeant, et dicat Bersabe regina;

Alas, God, for thy great pity
And for the might that is in thee,
Behold, I woful Bersabe
Cry out with stoopings of my knee
And thy wrath laid and bound on me
    Till I may see thy love.
Behold, Lord, this child is grown
Within me between bone and bone
To make me mother of a son,
Made of my body with strong moan;
There shall not be another one
    That shall be made hereof.

KING DAVID

Lord God, alas, what shall I sain?
Lo, thou art as an hundred men
Both to break and build again:
The wild ways thou makest plain,
Thine hands hold the hail and rain,
And thy fingers both grape and grain;
Of their largess we be all well fain,
    And of their great pity:
The sun thou madest of good gold,
Of clean silver the moon cold,
All the great stars thou hast told
As thy cattle in thy fold
Every one by his name of old;
Wind and water thou hast in hold,
    Both the land and the long sea;
Both the green sea and the land,
Lord God, thou hast in hand,
Both white water and grey sand;
Upon thy right or thy left hand
There is no man that may stand;
    Lord, thou rue on me.
O wise Lord, if thou be keen
To note things amiss that been,
I am not worth a shell of bean
More than an old mare meagre and lean;
For all my wrong-doing with my queen,
It grew not of our heartès clean,
    But it began of her body.
For it fell in the hot May
I stood within a paven way
Built of fair bright stone, perfay,
That is as fire of night and day
    And lighteth all my house.
Therein be neither stones nor sticks,
Neither red nor white bricks,
But for cubits five or six

There is most goodly sardonyx
   And amber laid in rows.
It goes round about my roofs,
(If ye list ye shall have proofs)
There is good space for horse and hoofs,
   Plain and nothing perilous.
For the fair green weather's heat,
And for the smell of leavès sweet,
It is no marvel, well ye weet,
   A man to waxen amorous.
This I say now by my case
That spied forth of that royal place;
There I saw in no great space
Mine own sweet, both body and face,
Under the fresh boughs.
In a water that was there
She wesshe her goodly body bare
And dried it with her owen hair:
Both her arms and her knees fair,
   Both bosom and brows;
Both shoulders and eke thighs
Tho she wesshe upon this wise;
Ever she sighed with little sighs,
   And ever she gave God thank.
Yea, God wot I can well see yet
Both her breast and her sides all wet
And her long hair withouten let
Spread sideways like a drawing net;
Full dear bought and full far fet
Was that sweet thing there y-set;
It were a hard thing to forget
How both lips and eyen met,
   Breast and breath sank.
So goodly a sight as there she was,
Lying looking on her glass
By wan water in green grass,

Yet saw never man.
So soft and great she was and bright
With all her body waxen white,
I woxe nigh blind to see the light
Shed out of it to left and right;
This bitter sin from that sweet sight
   Between us twain began.

NATHAN

Now, sir, be merry anon,
For ye shall have a full wise son,
Goodly and great of flesh and bone;
There shall no king be such an one,
   I swear by Godis rood.
Therefore, lord, be merry here,
And go to meat withouten fear,
And hear a mass with goodly cheer;
For to all folk ye shall be dear,
   And all folk of your blood.

   Et tunc dicant Laudamus.

ST. DOROTHY

It hath been seen and yet it shall be seen
  That out of tender mouths God's praise hath been
  Made perfect, and with wood and simple string
  He hath played music sweet as shawm-playing
  To please himself with softness of all sound;
  And no small thing but hath been sometime found
  Full sweet of use, and no such humbleness
  But God hath bruised withal the sentences
  And evidence of wise men witnessing;
  No leaf that is so soft a hidden thing
  It never shall get sight of the great sun;
  The strength of ten has been the strength of one,
  And lowliness has waxed imperious.
  There was in Rome a man Theophilus
Of right great blood and gracious ways, that had
All noble fashions to make people glad
And a soft life of pleasurable days;
He was a goodly man for one to praise,
Flawless and whole upward from foot to head;
His arms were a red hawk that alway fed
On a small bird with feathers gnawed upon,
Beaten and plucked about the bosom-bone
Whereby a small round fleck like fire there was:
They called it in their tongue lampadias;
This was the banner of the lordly man.
In many straits of sea and reaches wan
Full of quick wind, and many a shaken firth,
It had seen fighting days of either earth,
Westward or east of waters Gaditane
(This was the place of sea-rocks under Spain
Called after the great praise of Hercules)
And north beyond the washing Pontic seas,
Far windy Russian places fabulous,
And salt fierce tides of storm-swoln Bosphorus.

Now as this lord came straying in Rome town
He saw a little lattice open down
And after it a press of maidens' heads
That sat upon their cold small quiet beds
Talking, and played upon short-stringed lutes;
And other some ground perfume out of roots
Gathered by marvellous moons in Asia;
Saffron and aloes and wild cassia,
Coloured all through and smelling of the sun;
And over all these was a certain one
Clothed softly, with sweet herbs about her hair
And bosom flowerful; her face more fair
Than sudden-singing April in soft lands:
Eyed like a gracious bird, and in both hands
She held a psalter painted green and red.
  This Theophile laughed at the heart, and said,
Now God so help me hither and St. Paul,
As by the new time of their festival
I have good will to take this maid to wife.
And herewith fell to fancies of her life
And soft half-thoughts that ended suddenly.
This is man's guise to please himself, when he
Shall not see one thing of his pleasant things,
Nor with outwatch of many travailings
Come to be eased of the least pain he hath
For all his love and all his foolish wrath
And all the heavy manner of his mind.
Thus is he like a fisher fallen blind
That casts his nets across the boat awry
To strike the sea, but lo, he striketh dry
And plucks them back all broken for his pain
And bites his beard and casts across again
And reaching wrong slips over in the sea.
So hath this man a strangled neck for fee,
For all his cost he chuckles in his throat.
  This Theophile that little hereof wote

Laid wait to hear of her what she might be:
Men told him she had name of Dorothy,
And was a lady of a worthy house.
Thereat this knight grew inly glorious
That he should have a love so fair of place.
She was a maiden of most quiet face,
Tender of speech, and had no hardihood
But was nigh feeble of her fearful blood;
Her mercy in her was so marvellous
From her least years, that seeing her school-fellows
That read beside her stricken with a rod,
She would cry sore and say some word to God
That he would ease her fellow of his pain.
There is no touch of sun or fallen rain
That ever fell on a more gracious thing.
  In middle Rome there was in stone-working
The church of Venus painted royally.
The chapels of it were some two or three,
In each of them her tabernacle was
And a wide window of six feet in glass
Coloured with all her works in red and gold.
The altars had bright cloths and cups to hold
The wine of Venus for the services,
Made out of honey and crushed wood-berries
That shed sweet yellow through the thick wet red,
That on high days was borne upon the head
Of Venus' priest for any man to drink;
So that in drinking he should fall to think
On some fair face, and in the thought thereof
Worship, and such should triumph in his love.
For this soft wine that did such grace and good
Was new trans-shaped and mixed with Love's own blood,
That in the fighting Trojan time was bled;
For which came such a woe to Diomed
That he was stifled after in hard sea.
And some said that this wine-shedding should be

Made of the falling of Adonis' blood,
That curled upon the thorns and broken wood
And round the gold silk shoes on Venus' feet;
The taste thereof was as hot honey sweet
And in the mouth ran soft and riotous.
This was the holiness of Venus' house.
  It was their worship, that in August days
Twelve maidens should go through those Roman ways
Naked, and having gold across their brows
And their hair twisted in short golden rows,
To minister to Venus in this wise:
And twelve men chosen in their companies
To match these maidens by the altar-stair,
All in one habit, crowned upon the hair.
Among these men was chosen Theophile.
  This knight went out and prayed a little while,
Holding queen Venus by her hands and knees;
I will give thee twelve royal images
Cut in glad gold, with marvels of wrought stone
For thy sweet priests to lean and pray upon,
Jasper and hyacinth and chrysopras,
And the strange Asian thalamite that was
Hidden twelve ages under heavy sea
Among the little sleepy pearls, to be
A shrine lit over with soft candle-flame
Burning all night red as hot brows of shame,
So thou wilt be my lady without sin.
Goddess that art all gold outside and in,
Help me to serve thee in thy holy way.
Thou knowest, Love, that in my bearing day
There shone a laughter in the singing stars
Round the gold-ceiled bride-bed wherein Mars
Touched thee and had thee in your kissing wise.
Now therefore, sweet, kiss thou my maiden's eyes
That they may open graciously towards me;
And this new fashion of thy shrine shall be

As soft with gold as thine own happy head.
  The goddess, that was painted with face red
Between two long green tumbled sides of sea,
Stooped her neck sideways, and spake pleasantly:
Thou shalt have grace as thou art thrall of mine.
And with this came a savour of shed wine
And plucked-out petals from a rose's head:
And softly with slow laughs of lip she said,
Thou shalt have favour all thy days of me.
  Then came Theophilus to Dorothy,
Saying: O sweet, if one should strive or speak
Against God's ways, he gets a beaten cheek
For all his wage and shame above all men.
Therefore I have no will to turn again
When God saith "go," lest a worse thing fall out.
Then she, misdoubting lest he went about
To catch her wits, made answer somewhat thus:
I have no will, my lord Theophilus,
To speak against this worthy word of yours;
Knowing how God's will in all speech endures,
That save by grace there may no thing be said,
Then Theophile waxed light from foot to head,
And softly fell upon this answering.
It is well seen you are a chosen thing
To do God service in his gracious way.
I will that you make haste and holiday
To go next year upon the Venus stair,
Covered none else, but crowned upon your hair,
And do the service that a maiden doth.
She said: but I that am Christ's maid were loth
To do this thing that hath such bitter name.
Thereat his brows were beaten with sore shame
And he came off and said no other word.
Then his eyes chanced upon his banner-bird,
And he fell fingering at the staff of it
And laughed for wrath and stared between his feet,

And out of a chafed heart he spake as thus:
Lo how she japes at me Theophilus,
Feigning herself a fool and hard to love;
Yet in good time for all she boasteth of
She shall be like a little beaten bird.
And while his mouth was open in that word
He came upon the house Janiculum,
Where some went busily, and other some
Talked in the gate called the gate glorious.
The emperor, which was one Gabalus,
Sat over all and drank chill wine alone.
To whom is come Theophilus anon,
And said as thus: _Beau sire, Dieu vous aide_.
And afterward sat under him, and said
All this thing through as ye have wholly heard.
  This Gabalus laughed thickly in his beard.
Yea, this is righteousness and maiden rule.
Truly, he said, a maid is but a fool.
And japed at them as one full villainous,
In a lewd wise, this heathen Gabalus,
And sent his men to bind her as he bade.
Thus have they taken Dorothy the maid,
And haled her forth as men hale pick-purses:
A little need God knows they had of this,
To hale her by her maiden gentle hair.
Thus went she lowly, making a soft prayer,
As one who stays the sweet wine in his mouth,
Murmuring with eased lips, and is most loth
To have done wholly with the sweet of it.
  Christ king, fair Christ, that knowest all men's wit
And all the feeble fashion of my ways,
O perfect God, that from all yesterdays
Abidest whole with morrows perfected,
I pray thee by thy mother's holy head
Thou help me to do right, that I not slip:
I have no speech nor strength upon my lip,

Except thou help me who art wise and sweet.
Do this too for those nails that clove thy feet,
Let me die maiden after many pains.
Though I be least among thy handmaidens,
Doubtless I shall take death more sweetly thus.

  Now have they brought her to King Gabalus,
Who laughed in all his throat some breathing-whiles:
By God, he said, if one should leap two miles,
He were not pained about the sides so much.
This were a soft thing for a man to touch.
Shall one so chafe that hath such little bones?
And shook his throat with thick and chuckled moans
For laughter that she had such holiness.
What aileth thee, wilt thou do services?
It were good fare to fare as Venus doth.

  Then said this lady with her maiden mouth,
Shamefaced, and something paler in the cheek:
Now, sir, albeit my wit and will to speak
Give me no grace in sight of worthy men,
For all my shame yet know I this again,
I may not speak, nor after downlying
Rise up to take delight in lute-playing,
Nor sing nor sleep, nor sit and fold my hands,
But my soul in some measure understands
God's grace laid like a garment over me.
For this fair God that out of strong sharp sea
Lifted the shapely and green-coloured land,
And hath the weight of heaven in his hand
As one might hold a bird, and under him
The heavy golden planets beam by beam
Building the feasting-chambers of his house,
And the large world he holdeth with his brows,
And with the light of them astonisheth
All place and time and face of life and death
And motion of the north wind and the south,
And is the sound within his angel's mouth

Of singing words and words of thanksgiving,
And is the colour of the latter spring
And heat upon the summer and the sun,
And is beginning of all things begun
And gathers in him all things to their end,
And with the fingers of his hand doth bend
The stretched-out sides of heaven like a sail,
And with his breath he maketh the red pale
And fills with blood faint faces of men dead,
And with the sound between his lips are fed
Iron and fire and the white body of snow,
And blossom of all trees in places low,
And small bright herbs about the little hills,
And fruit pricked softly with birds' tender bills,
And flight of foam about green fields of sea,
And fourfold strength of the great winds that be
Moved always outward from beneath his feet,
And growth of grass and growth of sheaved wheat
And all green flower of goodly-growing lands;
And all these things he gathers with his hands
And covers all their beauty with his wings;
The same, even God that governs all these things,
Hath set my feet to be upon his ways.
Now therefore for no painfulness of days
I shall put off this service bound on me.
Also, fair sir, ye know this certainly,
How God was in his flesh full chaste and meek
And gave his face to shame, and either cheek
Gave up to smiting of men tyrannous.
 And here with a great voice this Gabalus
Cried out and said: By God's blood and his bones,
This were good game betwixen night and nones
For one to sit and hearken to such saws:
I were as lief fall in some big beast's jaws
As hear these women's jaw-teeth clattering;
By God a woman is the harder thing,

One may not put a hook into her mouth.
Now by St. Luke I am so sore adrouth
For all these saws I must needs drink again.
But I pray God deliver all us men
From all such noise of women and their heat.
That is a noble scripture, well I weet,
That likens women to an empty can;
When God said that he was a full wise man,
I trow no man may blame him as for that.
  And herewithal he drank a draught, and spat,
And said: Now shall I make an end hereof.
Come near all men and hearken for God's love,
And ye shall hear a jest or twain, God wot.
And spake as thus with mouth full thick and hot;
But thou do this thou shalt be shortly slain.
Lo, sir, she said, this death and all this pain
I take in penance of my bitter sins.
Yea now, quoth Gabalus, this game begins.
Lo, without sin one shall not live a span.
Lo, this is she that would not look on man
Between her fingers folded in thwart wise.
See how her shame hath smitten in her eyes
That was so clean she had not heard of shame.
Certes, he said, by Gabalus my name,
This two years back I was not so well pleased.
This were good mirth for sick men to be eased
And rise up whole and laugh at hearing of.
I pray thee show us something of thy love,
Since thou wast maid thy gown is waxen wide.
Yea, maid I am, she said, and somewhat sighed,
As one who thought upon the low fair house
Where she sat working, with soft bended brows
Watching her threads, among the school-maidens.
And she thought well now God had brought her thence
She should not come to sew her gold again.
  Then cried King Gabalus upon his men

To have her forth and draw her with steel gins.
And as a man hag-ridden beats and grins
And bends his body sidelong in his bed,
So wagged he with his body and knave's head,
Gaping at her, and blowing with his breath.
And in good time he gat an evil death
Out of his lewdness with his cursed wives:
His bones were hewn asunder as with knives
For his misliving, certes it is said.
But all the evil wrought upon this maid,
It were full hard for one to handle it.
For her soft blood was shed upon her feet,
And all her body's colour bruised and faint.
But she, as one abiding God's great saint,
Spake not nor wept for all this travail hard.
Wherefore the king commanded afterward
To slay her presently in all men's sight.
And it was now an hour upon the night
And winter-time, and a few stars began.
The weather was yet feeble and all wan
For beating of a weighty wind and snow.
And she came walking in soft wise and slow,
And many men with faces piteous.
Then came this heavy cursing Gabalus,
That swore full hard into his drunken beard;
And faintly after without any word
Came Theophile some paces off the king.
And in the middle of this wayfaring
Full tenderly beholding her he said:

  There is no word of comfort with men dead
Nor any face and colour of things sweet;
But always with lean cheeks and lifted feet
These dead men lie all aching to the blood
With bitter cold, their brows withouten hood
Beating for chill, their bodies swathed full thin:
Alas, what hire shall any have herein

To give his life and get such bitterness?
Also the soul going forth bodiless
Is hurt with naked cold, and no man saith
If there be house or covering for death
To hide the soul that is discomforted.
  Then she beholding him a little said:
Alas, fair lord, ye have no wit of this;
For on one side death is full poor of bliss
And as ye say full sharp of bone and lean:
But on the other side is good and green
And hath soft flower of tender-coloured hair
Grown on his head, and a red mouth as fair
As may be kissed with lips; thereto his face
Is as God's face, and in a perfect place
Full of all sun and colour of straight boughs
And waterheads about a painted house
That hath a mile of flowers either way
Outward from it, and blossom-grass of May
Thickening on many a side for length of heat,
Hath God set death upon a noble seat
Covered with green and flowered in the fold,
In likeness of a great king grown full old
And gentle with new temperance of blood;
And on his brows a purfled purple hood,
They may not carry any golden thing;
And plays some tune with subtle fingering
On a small cithern, full of tears and sleep
And heavy pleasure that is quick to weep
And sorrow with the honey in her mouth;
And for this might of music that he doth
Are all souls drawn toward him with great love
And weep for sweetness of the noise thereof
And bow to him with worship of their knees;
And all the field is thick with companies
Of fair-clothed men that play on shawms and lutes
And gather honey of the yellow fruits

Between the branches waxen soft and wide:
And all this peace endures in either side
Of the green land, and God beholdeth all.
And this is girdled with a round fair wall
Made of red stone and cool with heavy leaves
Grown out against it, and green blossom cleaves
To the green chinks, and lesser wall-weed sweet,
Kissing the crannies that are split with heat,
And branches where the summer draws to head.

  And Theophile burnt in the cheek, and said:
Yea, could one see it, this were marvellous.
I pray you, at your coming to this house,
Give me some leaf of all those tree-branches;
Seeing how so sharp and white our weather is,
There is no green nor gracious red to see.

  Yea, sir, she said, that shall I certainly.
And from her long sweet throat without a fleck
Undid the gold, and through her stretched-out neck
The cold axe clove, and smote away her head:
Out of her throat the tender blood full red
Fell suddenly through all her long soft hair.
And with good speed for hardness of the air
Each man departed to his house again.

  Lo, as fair colour in the face of men
At seed-time of their blood, or in such wise
As a thing seen increaseth in men's eyes,
Caught first far off by sickly fits of sight,
So a word said, if one shall hear aright,
Abides against the season of its growth.
This Theophile went slowly, as one doth
That is not sure for sickness of his feet;
And counting the white stonework of the street,
Tears fell out of his eyes for wrath and love,
Making him weep more for the shame thereof
Than for true pain: so went he half a mile.
And women mocked him, saying: Theophile,

Lo, she is dead; what shall a woman have
That loveth such an one? so Christ me save,
I were as lief to love a man new-hung.
Surely this man has bitten on his tongue,
This makes him sad and writhled in his face.

  And when they came upon the paven place
That was called sometime the place amorous
There came a child before Theophilus
Bearing a basket, and said suddenly:
Fair sir, this is my mistress Dorothy
That sends you gifts; and with this he was gone.
In all this earth there is not such an one
For colour and straight stature made so fair.
The tender growing gold of his pure hair
Was as wheat growing, and his mouth as flame.
God called him Holy after his own name;
With gold cloth like fire burning he was clad.
But for the fair green basket that he had,
It was filled up with heavy white and red;
Great roses stained still where the first rose bled,
Burning at heart for shame their heart withholds:
And the sad colour of strong marigolds
That have the sun to kiss their lips for love;
The flower that Venus' hair is woven of,
The colour of fair apples in the sun,
Late peaches gathered when the heat was done
And the slain air got breath; and after these
The fair faint-headed poppies drunk with ease,
And heaviness of hollow lilies red.

  Then cried they all that saw these things, and said
It was God's doing, and was marvellous.
And in brief while this knight Theophilus
Is waxen full of faith, and witnesseth
Before the king of God and love and death,
For which the king bade hang him presently.
A gallows of a goodly piece of tree

This Gabalus hath made to hang him on.
Forth of this world lo Theophile is gone
With a wried neck, God give us better fare
Than his that hath a twisted throat to wear;
But truly for his love God hath him brought
There where his heavy body grieves him nought
Nor all the people plucking at his feet;
But in his face his lady's face is sweet,
And through his lips her kissing lips are gone:
God send him peace, and joy of such an one.
  This is the story of St. Dorothy.
I will you of your mercy pray for me
Because I wrote these sayings for your grace,
That I may one day see her in the face.

THE TWO DREAMS

(FROM BOCCACCIO)

I will that if I say a heavy thing
Your tongues forgive me; seeing ye know that spring
Has flecks and fits of pain to keep her sweet,
And walks somewhile with winter-bitten feet.
Moreover it sounds often well to let
One string, when ye play music, keep at fret
The whole song through; one petal that is dead
Confirms the roses, be they white or red;
Dead sorrow is not sorrowful to hear
As the thick noise that breaks mid weeping were;
The sick sound aching in a lifted throat
Turns to sharp silver of a perfect note;
And though the rain falls often, and with rain
Late autumn falls on the old red leaves like pain,
I deem that God is not disquieted.
Also while men are fed with wine and bread,
They shall be fed with sorrow at his hand.
  There grew a rose-garden in Florence land
More fair than many; all red summers through
The leaves smelt sweet and sharp of rain, and blew
Sideways with tender wind; and therein fell
Sweet sound wherewith the green waxed audible,
As a bird's will to sing disturbed his throat
And set the sharp wings forward like a boat
Pushed through soft water, moving his brown side
Smooth-shapen as a maid's, and shook with pride
His deep warm bosom, till the heavy sun's
Set face of heat stopped all the songs at once.
The ways were clean to walk and delicate;
And when the windy white of March grew late,
Before the trees took heart to face the sun

With ravelled raiment of lean winter on,
The roots were thick and hot with hollow grass.
  Some roods away a lordly house there was,
Cool with broad courts and latticed passage wet
From rush-flowers and lilies ripe to set,
Sown close among the strewings of the floor;
And either wall of the slow corridor
Was dim with deep device of gracious things;
Some angel's steady mouth and weight of wings
Shut to the side; or Peter with straight stole
And beard cut black against the aureole
That spanned his head from nape to crown; thereby
Mary's gold hair, thick to the girdle-tie
Wherein was bound a child with tender feet;
Or the broad cross with blood nigh brown on it.
  Within this house a righteous lord abode,
Ser Averardo; patient of his mood,
And just of judgment; and to child he had
A maid so sweet that her mere sight made glad
Men sorrowing, and unbound the brows of hate;
And where she came, the lips that pain made strait
Waxed warm and wide, and from untender grew
Tender as those that sleep brings patience to.
Such long locks had she, that with knee to chin
She might have wrapped and warmed her feet therein.
Right seldom fell her face on weeping wise;
Gold hair she had, and golden-coloured eyes,
Filled with clear light and fire and large repose
Like a fair hound's; no man there is but knows
Her face was white, and thereto she was tall;
In no wise lacked there any praise at all
To her most perfect and pure maidenhood;
No sin I think there was in all her blood.
  She, where a gold grate shut the roses in,
Dwelt daily through deep summer weeks, through green
Flushed hours of rain upon the leaves; and there

Love made him room and space to worship her
With tender worship of bowed knees, and wrought
Such pleasure as the pained sense palates not
For weariness, but at one taste undoes
The heart of its strong sweet, is ravenous
Of all the hidden honey; words and sense
Fail through the tune's imperious prevalence.
 In a poor house this lover kept apart,
Long communing with patience next his heart
If love of his might move that face at all,
Tuned evenwise with colours musical;
Then after length of days he said thus: "Love,
For love's own sake and for the love thereof
Let no harsh words untune your gracious mood;
For good it were, if anything be good,
To comfort me in this pain's plague of mine;
Seeing thus, how neither sleep nor bread nor wine
Seems pleasant to me, yea no thing that is
Seems pleasant to me; only I know this,
Love's ways are sharp for palms of piteous feet
To travel, but the end of such is sweet:
Now do with me as seemeth you the best."
She mused a little, as one holds his guest
By the hand musing, with her face borne down:
Then said: "Yea, though such bitter seed be sown,
Have no more care of all that you have said;
Since if there is no sleep will bind your head,
Lo, I am fain to help you certainly;
Christ knoweth, sir, if I would have you die;
There is no pleasure when a man is dead."
Thereat he kissed her hands and yellow head
And clipped her fair long body many times;
I have no wit to shape in written rhymes
A scanted tithe of this great joy they had.
 They were too near love's secret to be glad;
As whoso deems the core will surely melt

From the warm fruit his lips caress, hath felt
Some bitter kernel where the teeth shut hard:
Or as sweet music sharpens afterward,
Being half disrelished both for sharp and sweet;
As sea-water, having killed over-heat
In a man's body, chills it with faint ache;
So their sense, burdened only for love's sake,
Failed for pure love; yet so time served their wit,
They saved each day some gold reserves of it,
Being wiser in love's riddle than such be
Whom fragments feed with his chance charity.
All things felt sweet were felt sweet overmuch;
The rose-thorn's prickle dangerous to touch,
And flecks of fire in the thin leaf-shadows;
Too keen the breathed honey of the rose,
Its red too harsh a weight on feasted eyes;
They were so far gone in love's histories,
Beyond all shape and colour and mere breath,
Where pleasure has for kinsfolk sleep and death,
And strength of soul and body waxen blind
For weariness, and flesh entailed with mind,
When the keen edge of sense foretasteth sin.
  Even this green place the summer caught them in
Seemed half deflowered and sick with beaten leaves
In their strayed eyes; these gold flower-fumèd eves
Burnt out to make the sun's love-offering,
The midnoon's prayer, the rose's thanksgiving,
The trees' weight burdening the strengthless air,
The shape of her stilled eyes, her coloured hair,
Her body's balance from the moving feet--
All this, found fair, lacked yet one grain of sweet
It had some warm weeks back: so perisheth
On May's new lip the tender April breath:
So those same walks the wind sowed lilies in
All April through, and all their latter kin
Of languid leaves whereon the Autumn blows--

The dead red raiment of the last year's rose--
The last year's laurel, and the last year's love,
Fade, and grow things that death grows weary of.
 What man will gather in red summer-time
The fruit of some obscure and hoary rhyme
Heard last midwinter, taste the heart in it,
Mould the smooth semitones afresh, refit
The fair limbs ruined, flush the dead blood through
With colour, make all broken beauties new
For love's new lesson--shall not such find pain
When the marred music labouring in his brain
Frets him with sweet sharp fragments, and lets slip
One word that might leave satisfied his lip--
One touch that might put fire in all the chords?
This was her pain: to miss from all sweet words
Some taste of sound, diverse and delicate--
Some speech the old love found out to compensate
For seasons of shut lips and drowsiness--
Some grace, some word the old love found out to bless
Passionless months and undelighted weeks.
The flowers had lost their summer-scented cheeks,
Their lips were no more sweet than daily breath:
The year was plagued with instances of death.
 So fell it, these were sitting in cool grass
With leaves about, and many a bird there was
Where the green shadow thickliest impleached
Soft fruit and writhen spray and blossom bleached
Dry in the sun or washed with rains to white:
Her girdle was pure silk, the bosom bright
With purple as purple water and gold wrought in.
One branch had touched with dusk her lips and chin,
Made violet of the throat, abashed with shade
The breast's bright plaited work: but nothing frayed
The sun's large kiss on the luxurious hair.
Her beauty was new colour to the air
And music to the silent many birds.

Love was an-hungred for some perfect words
To praise her with; but only her low name
"Andrevuola" came thrice, and thrice put shame
In her clear cheek, so fruitful with new red
That for pure love straightway shame's self was dead.
  Then with lids gathered as who late had wept
She began saying: "I have so little slept
My lids drowse now against the very sun;
Yea, the brain aching with a dream begun
Beats like a fitful blood; kiss but both brows,
And you shall pluck my thoughts grown dangerous
Almost away." He said thus, kissing them:
"O sole sweet thing that God is glad to name,
My one gold gift, if dreams be sharp and sore
Shall not the waking time increase much more
With taste and sound, sweet eyesight or sweet scent?
Has any heat too hard and insolent
Burnt bare the tender married leaves, undone
The maiden grass shut under from the sun?
Where in this world is room enough for pain?"
  The feverish finger of love had touched again
Her lips with happier blood; the pain lay meek
In her fair face, nor altered lip nor cheek
With pallor or with pulse; but in her mouth
Love thirsted as a man wayfaring doth,
Making it humble as weak hunger is.
She lay close to him, bade do this and this,
Say that, sing thus: then almost weeping-ripe
Crouched, then laughed low. As one that fain would wipe
The old record out of old things done and dead,
She rose, she heaved her hands up, and waxed red
For wilful heart and blameless fear of blame;
Saying "Though my wits be weak, this is no shame
For a poor maid whom love so punisheth
With heats of hesitation and stopped breath
That with my dreams I live yet heavily

For pure sad heart and faith's humility.
Now be not wroth and I will show you this.
  "Methought our lips upon their second kiss
Met in this place, and a fair day we had
And fair soft leaves that waxed and were not sad
With shaken rain or bitten through with drouth;
When I, beholding ever how your mouth
Waited for mine, the throat being fallen back,
Saw crawl thereout a live thing flaked with black
Specks of brute slime and leper-coloured scale,
A devil's hide with foul flame-writhen grail
Fashioned where hell's heat festers loathsomest;
And that brief speech may ease me of the rest,
Thus were you slain and eaten of the thing.
My waked eyes felt the new day shuddering
On their low lids, felt the whole east so beat,
Pant with close pulse of such a plague-struck heat,
As if the palpitating dawn drew breath
For horror, breathing between life and death,
Till the sun sprang blood-bright and violent."
  So finishing, her soft strength wholly spent,
She gazed each way, lest some brute-hoovèd thing,
The timeless travail of hell's childbearing,
Should threat upon the sudden: whereat he,
For relish of her tasted misery
And tender little thornprick of her pain,
Laughed with mere love. What lover among men
But hath his sense fed sovereignly 'twixt whiles
With tears and covered eyelids and sick smiles
And soft disaster of a painèd face?
What pain, established in so sweet a place,
But the plucked leaf of it smells fragrantly?
What colour burning man's wide-open eye
But may be pleasurably seen? what sense
Keeps in its hot sharp extreme violence
No savour of sweet things? The bereaved blood

And emptied flesh in their most broken mood
Fail not so wholly, famish not when thus
Past honey keeps the starved lip covetous.
  Therefore this speech from a glad mouth began,
Breathed in her tender hair and temples wan
Like one prolonged kiss while the lips had breath.
"Sleep, that abides in vassalage of death
And in death's service wears out half his age,
Hath his dreams full of deadly vassalage,
Shadow and sound of things ungracious;
Fair shallow faces, hooded bloodless brows,
And mouths past kissing; yea, myself have had
As harsh a dream as holds your eyelids sad.
  "This dream I tell you came three nights ago;
In full mid sleep I took a whim to know
How sweet things might be; so I turned and thought;
But save my dream all sweet availed me not.
First came a smell of pounded spice and scent
Such as God ripens in some continent
Of utmost amber in the Syrian sea;
And breaths as though some costly rose could be
Spoiled slowly, wasted by some bitter fire
To burn the sweet out leaf by leaf, and tire
The flower's poor heart with heat and waste, to make
Strong magic for some perfumed woman's sake.
Then a cool naked sense beneath my feet
Of bud and blossom; and sound of veins that beat
As if a lute should play of its own heart
And fearfully, not smitten of either part;
And all my blood it filled with sharp and sweet
As gold swoln grain fills out the huskèd wheat;
So I rose naked from the bed, and stood
Counting the mobile measure in my blood
Some pleasant while, and through each limb there came
Swift little pleasures pungent as a flame,
Felt in the thrilling flesh and veins as much

As the outer curls that feel the comb's first touch
Thrill to the roots and shiver as from fire;
And blind between my dream and my desire
I seemed to stand and held my spirit still
Lest this should cease. A child whose fingers spill
Honey from cells forgotten of the bee
Is less afraid to stir the hive and see
Some wasp's bright back inside, than I to feel
Some finger-touch disturb the flesh like steel.
I prayed thus; Let me catch a secret here
So sweet, it sharpens the sweet taste of fear
And takes the mouth with edge of wine; I would
Have here some colour and smooth shape as good
As those in heaven whom the chief garden hides
With low grape-blossom veiling their white sides
And lesser tendrils that so bind and blind
Their eyes and feet, that if one come behind
To touch their hair they see not, neither fly;
This would I see in heaven and not die.
So praying, I had nigh cried out and knelt,
So wholly my prayer filled me: till I felt
In the dumb night's warm weight of glowing gloom
Somewhat that altered all my sleeping-room,
And made it like a green low place wherein
Maids mix to bathe: one sets her small warm chin
Against a ripple, that the angry pearl
May flow like flame about her: the next curl
Dips in some eddy coloured of the sun
To wash the dust well out; another one
Holds a straight ankle in her hand and swings
With lavish body sidelong, so that rings
Of sweet fierce water, swollen and splendid, fail
All round her fine and floated body pale,
Swayed flower-fashion, and her balanced side
Swerved edgeways lets the weight of water slide,
As taken in some underflow of sea

Swerves the banked gold of sea-flowers; but she
Pulls down some branch to keep her perfect head
Clear of the river: even from wall to bed,
I tell you, was my room transfigured so.
Sweet, green and warm it was, nor could one know
If there were walls or leaves, or if there was
No bed's green curtain, but mere gentle grass.
There were set also hard against the feet
Gold plates with honey and green grapes to eat,
With the cool water's noise to hear in rhymes:
And a wind warmed me full of furze and limes
And all hot sweets the heavy summer fills
To the round brim of smooth cup-shapen hills.
Next the grave walking of a woman's feet
Made my veins hesitate, and gracious heat
Made thick the lids and leaden on mine eyes:
And I thought ever, surely it were wise
Not yet to see her: this may last (who knows?)
Five minutes; the poor rose is twice a rose
Because it turns a face to her, the wind
Sings that way; hath this woman ever sinned,
I wonder? as a boy with apple-rind,
I played with pleasures, made them to my mind,
Changed each ere tasting. When she came indeed,
First her hair touched me, then I grew to feed
On the sense of her hand; her mouth at last
Touched me between the cheek and lip and past
Over my face with kisses here and there
Sown in and out across the eyes and hair.
Still I said nothing; till she set her face
More close and harder on the kissing-place,
And her mouth caught like a snake's mouth, and stung
So faint and tenderly, the fang scarce clung
More than a bird's foot: yet a wound it grew,
A great one, let this red mark witness you
Under the left breast; and the stroke thereof

So clove my sense that I woke out of love
And knew not what this dream was nor had wit;
But now God knows if I have skill of it."
  Hereat she laid one palm against her lips
To stop their trembling; as when water slips
Out of a beak-mouthed vessel with faint noise
And chuckles in the narrowed throat and cloys
The carven rims with murmuring, so came
Words in her lips with no word right of them,
A beaten speech thick and disconsolate,
Till his smile ceasing waxed compassionate
Of her sore fear that grew from anything--
The sound of the strong summer thickening
In heated leaves of the smooth apple-trees:
The day's breath felt about the ash-branches,
And noises of the noon whose weight still grew
On the hot heavy-headed flowers, and drew
Their red mouths open till the rose-heart ached;
For eastward all the crowding rose was slaked
And soothed with shade: but westward all its growth
Seemed to breathe hard with heat as a man doth
Who feels his temples newly feverous.
And even with such motion in her brows
As that man hath in whom sick days begin,
She turned her throat and spake, her voice being thin
As a sick man's, sudden and tremulous;
"Sweet, if this end be come indeed on us,
Let us love more;" and held his mouth with hers.
As the first sound of flooded hill-waters
Is heard by people of the meadow-grass,
Or ever a wandering waif of ruin pass
With whirling stones and foam of the brown stream
Flaked with fierce yellow: so beholding him
She felt before tears came her eyelids wet,
Saw the face deadly thin where life was yet,
Heard his throat's harsh last moan before it clomb:

And he, with close mouth passionate and dumb,
Burned at her lips: so lay they without speech,
Each grasping other, and the eyes of each
Fed in the other's face: till suddenly
He cried out with a little broken cry
This word, "O help me, sweet, I am but dead."
And even so saying, the colour of fair red
Was gone out of his face, and his blood's beat
Fell, and stark death made sharp his upward feet
And pointed hands; and without moan he died.
Pain smote her sudden in the brows and side,
Strained her lips open and made burn her eyes:
For the pure sharpness of her miseries
She had no heart's pain, but mere body's wrack;
But at the last her beaten blood drew back
Slowly upon her face, and her stunned brows
Suddenly grown aware and piteous
Gathered themselves, her eyes shone, her hard breath
Came as though one nigh dead came back from death;
Her lips throbbed, and life trembled through her hair.
 And in brief while she thought to bury there
The dead man that her love might lie with him
In a sweet bed under the rose-roots dim
And soft earth round the branchèd apple-trees,
Full of hushed heat and heavy with great ease,
And no man entering divide him thence.
Wherefore she bade one of her handmaidens
To be her help to do upon this wise.
And saying so the tears out of her eyes
Fell without noise and comforted her heart:
Yea, her great pain eased of the sorest part
Began to soften in her sense of it.
There under all the little branches sweet
The place was shapen of his burial;
They shed thereon no thing funereal,
But coloured leaves of latter rose-blossom,

Stems of soft grass, some withered red and some
Fair and fresh-blooded; and spoil splendider
Of marigold and great spent sunflower.
  And afterward she came back without word
To her own house; two days went, and the third
Went, and she showed her father of this thing.
And for great grief of her soul's travailing
He gave consent she should endure in peace
Till her life's end; yea, till her time should cease,
She should abide in fellowship of pain.
And having lived a holy year or twain
She died of pure waste heart and weariness.
And for love's honour in her love's distress
This word was written over her tomb's head;
"Here dead she lieth, for whose sake Love is dead."

AHOLIBAH

In the beginning God made thee
   A woman well to look upon,
Thy tender body as a tree
   Whereon cool wind hath always blown
   Till the clean branches be well grown.

There was none like thee in the land;
   The girls that were thy bondwomen
Did bind thee with a purple band
   Upon thy forehead, that all men
   Should know thee for God's handmaiden.

Strange raiment clad thee like a bride,
   With silk to wear on hands and feet
And plates of gold on either side:
   Wine made thee glad, and thou didst eat
   Honey, and choice of pleasant meat.

And fishers in the middle sea
   Did get thee sea-fish and sea-weeds
In colour like the robes on thee;
   And curious work of plaited reeds,
   And wools wherein live purple bleeds.

And round the edges of thy cup
   Men wrought thee marvels out of gold,
Strong snakes with lean throats lifted up,
   Large eyes whereon the brows had hold,
   And scaly things their slime kept cold.

For thee they blew soft wind in flutes
   And ground sweet roots for cunning scent;

Made slow because of many lutes,
    The wind among thy chambers went
    Wherein no light was violent.

God called thy name Aholibah,
    His tabernacle being in thee,
A witness through waste Asia;
    Thou wert a tent sewn cunningly
    With gold and colours of the sea.

God gave thee gracious ministers
    And all their work who plait and weave:
The cunning of embroiderers
    That sew the pillow to the sleeve,
    And likeness of all things that live.

Thy garments upon thee were fair
    With scarlet and with yellow thread;
Also the weaving of thine hair
    Was as fine gold upon thy head,
    And thy silk shoes were sewn with red.

All sweet things he bade sift, and ground
    As a man grindeth wheat in mills
With strong wheels alway going round;
    He gave thee corn, and grass that fills
    The cattle on a thousand hills.

The wine of many seasons fed
    Thy mouth, and made it fair and clean;
Sweet oil was poured out on thy head
    And ran down like cool rain between
    The strait close locks it melted in.

The strong men and the captains knew
    Thy chambers wrought and fashioned

With gold and covering of blue,
   And the blue raiment of thine head
   Who satest on a stately bed.

All these had on their garments wrought
   The shape of beasts and creeping things,
The body that availeth not,
   Flat backs of worms and veinèd wings,
   And the lewd bulk that sleeps and stings.

Also the chosen of the years,
   The multitude being at ease,
With sackbuts and with dulcimers
   And noise of shawms and psalteries
   Made mirth within the ears of these.

But as a common woman doth,
   Thou didst think evil and devise;
The sweet smell of thy breast and mouth
   Thou madest as the harlot's wise,
   And there was painting on thine eyes.

Yea, in the woven guest-chamber
   And by the painted passages
Where the strange gracious paintings were,
   State upon state of companies,
   There came on thee the lust of these.

Because of shapes on either wall
   Sea-coloured from some rare blue shell
At many a Tyrian interval,

Horsemen on horses, girdled well,
   Delicate and desirable,

Thou saidest: I am sick of love:

Stay me with flagons, comfort me
With apples for my pain thereof
   Till my hands gather in his tree
   That fruit wherein my lips would be.

Yea, saidest thou, I will go up
   When there is no more shade than one
May cover with a hollow cup,
   And make my bed against the sun
   Till my blood's violence be done.

Thy mouth was leant upon the wall
   Against the painted mouth, thy chin
Touched the hair's painted curve and fall;
   Thy deep throat, fallen lax and thin,
   Worked as the blood's beat worked therein.

Therefore, O thou Aholibah,
   God is not glad because of thee;
And thy fine gold shall pass away
   Like those fair coins of ore that be
   Washed over by the middle sea.

Then will one make thy body bare
   To strip it of all gracious things,
And pluck the cover from thine hair,
   And break the gift of many kings,
   Thy wrist-rings and thine ankle-rings.

Likewise the man whose body joins
   To thy smooth body, as was said,
Who hath a girdle on his loins
   And dyed attire upon his head--
   The same who, seeing, worshipped,

Because thy face was like the face

Of a clean maiden that smells sweet,
Because thy gait was as the pace
    Of one that opens not her feet
    And is not heard within the street--

Even he, O thou Aholibah,
    Made separate from thy desire,
Shall cut thy nose and ears away
    And bruise thee for thy body's hire
    And burn the residue with fire.

Then shall the heathen people say,
    The multitude being at ease;
Lo, this is that Aholibah
    Whose name was blown among strange seas.
    Grown old with soft adulteries.

Also her bed was made of green,
    Her windows beautiful for glass
That she had made her bed between:
    Yea, for pure lust her body was
    Made like white summer-coloured grass.

Her raiment was a strong man's spoil;
    Upon a table by a bed
She set mine incense and mine oil
    To be the beauty of her head
    In chambers walled about with red.

Also between the walls she had
    Fair faces of strong men portrayed;
All girded round the loins, and clad
    With several cloths of woven braid
    And garments marvellously made.

Therefore the wrath of God shall be
    Set as a watch upon her way;
And whoso findeth by the sea
    Blown dust of bones will hardly say
    If this were that Aholibah.

LOVE AND SLEEP

Lying asleep between the strokes of night
  I saw my love lean over my sad bed,
  Pale as the duskiest lily's leaf or head,
Smooth-skinned and dark, with bare throat made to bite,
Too wan for blushing and too warm for white,
  But perfect-coloured without white or red.
  And her lips opened amorously, and said--
I wist not what, saving one word--Delight.
And all her face was honey to my mouth,
  And all her body pasture to mine eyes;
    The long lithe arms and hotter hands than fire,
The quivering flanks, hair smelling of the south,
  The bright light feet, the splendid supple thighs
    And glittering eyelids of my soul's desire.

MADONNA MIA

Under green apple-boughs
That never a storm will rouse,
My lady hath her house
  Between two bowers;
In either of the twain
Red roses full of rain;
She hath for bondwomen
  All kind of flowers.

She hath no handmaid fair
To draw her curled gold hair
Through rings of gold that bear
  Her whole hair's weight;
She hath no maids to stand
Gold-clothed on either hand;
In all the great green land
  None is so great.

She hath no more to wear
But one white hood of vair
Drawn over eyes and hair,
  Wrought with strange gold,
Made for some great queen's head,
Some fair great queen since dead;
And one strait gown of red
  Against the cold.

Beneath her eyelids deep
Love lying seems asleep,
Love, swift to wake, to weep,
  To laugh, to gaze;
Her breasts are like white birds,
And all her gracious words
As water-grass to herds

In the June-days.

To her all dews that fall
And rains are musical;
Her flowers are fed from all,
  Her joy from these;
In the deep-feathered firs
Their gift of joy is hers,
In the least breath that stirs
  Across the trees.

She grows with greenest leaves,
Ripens with reddest sheaves,
Forgets, remembers, grieves,
  And is not sad;
The quiet lands and skies
Leave light upon her eyes;
None knows her, weak or wise,
  Or tired or glad.

None knows, none understands,
What flowers are like her hands;
Though you should search all lands
  Wherein time grows,
What snows are like her feet,
Though his eyes burn with heat
Through gazing on my sweet,
  Yet no man knows.

Only this thing is said;
That white and gold and red,
God's three chief words, man's bread
  And oil and wine,
Were given her for dowers,
And kingdom of all hours,
And grace of goodly flowers

   And various vine.

This is my lady's praise:
God after many days
Wrought her in unknown ways,
  In sunset lands;
This was my lady's birth;
God gave her might and mirth
And laid his whole sweet earth
  Between her hands.

Under deep apple-boughs
My lady hath her house;
She wears upon her brows
  The flower thereof;
All saying but what God saith
To her is as vain breath;
She is more strong than death,
  Being strong as love.

THE KING'S DAUGHTER

We were ten maidens in the green corn,
  Small red leaves in the mill-water:
Fairer maidens never were born,
  Apples of gold for the king's daughter.

We were ten maidens by a well-head,
  Small white birds in the mill-water:
Sweeter maidens never were wed,
  Rings of red for the king's daughter.

The first to spin, the second to sing,
  Seeds of wheat in the mill-water;
The third may was a goodly thing,
  White bread and brown for the king's daughter.

The fourth to sew and the fifth to play,
  Fair green weed in the mill-water;
The sixth may was a goodly may,
  White wine and red for the king's daughter.

The seventh to woo, the eighth to wed,
  Fair thin reeds in the mill-water;
The ninth had gold work on her head,
  Honey in the comb for the king's daughter.

The ninth had gold work round her hair,
  Fallen flowers in the mill-water;
The tenth may was goodly and fair,
  Golden gloves for the king's daughter.

We were ten maidens in a field green,
  Fallen fruit in the mill-water;
Fairer maidens never have been,
  Golden sleeves for the king's daughter.

By there comes the king's young son,
  A little wind in the mill-water;
"Out of ten maidens ye'll grant me one,"
  A crown of red for the king's daughter.

"Out of ten mays ye'll give me the best,"
  A little rain in the mill-water;
A bed of yellow straw for all the rest,
  A bed of gold for the king's daughter.

He's ta'en out the goodliest,
  Rain that rains in the mill-water;
A comb of yellow shell for all the rest,
  A comb of gold for the king's daughter.

He's made her bed to the goodliest,
  Wind and hail in the mill-water;
A grass girdle for all the rest,
  A girdle of arms for the king's daughter.

He's set his heart to the goodliest,
  Snow that snows in the mill-water;
Nine little kisses for all the rest,
  An hundredfold for the king's daughter.

He's ta'en his leave at the goodliest,
  Broken boats in the mill-water;
Golden gifts for all the rest,
  Sorrow of heart for the king's daughter.

"Ye'll make a grave for my fair body,"
  Running rain in the mill-water;
"And ye'll streek my brother at the side of me,"
  The pains of hell for the king's daughter.

AFTER DEATH

The four boards of the coffin lid
Heard all the dead man did.

The first curse was in his mouth,
Made of grave's mould and deadly drouth.

The next curse was in his head,
Made of God's work discomfited.

The next curse was in his hands,
Made out of two grave-bands.

The next curse was in his feet,
Made out of a grave-sheet.

"I had fair coins red and white,
And my name was as great light;

I had fair clothes green and red,
And strong gold bound round my head.

But no meat comes in my mouth,
Now I fare as the worm doth;

And no gold binds in my hair,
Now I fare as the blind fare.

My live thews were of great strength,
Now am I waxen a span's length;

My live sides were full of lust,
Now are they dried with dust."

The first board spake and said:
"Is it best eating flesh or bread?"

The second answered it:
"Is wine or honey the more sweet?"

The third board spake and said:
"Is red gold worth a girl's gold head?"

The fourth made answer thus:
"All these things are as one with us."

The dead man asked of them:
"Is the green land stained brown with flame?

Have they hewn my son for beasts to eat,
And my wife's body for beasts' meat?

Have they boiled my maid in a brass pan,
And built a gallows to hang my man?"

The boards said to him:
"This is a lewd thing that ye deem.

Your wife has gotten a golden bed,
All the sheets are sewn with red.

Your son has gotten a coat of silk,
The sleeves are soft as curded milk.

Your maid has gotten a kirtle new,
All the skirt has braids of blue.

Your man has gotten both ring and glove,
Wrought well for eyes to love."

The dead man answered thus:
"What good gift shall God give us?"

The boards answered him anon:
"Flesh to feed hell's worm upon."

MAY JANET

(BRETON)

"Stand up, stand up, thou May Janet,
  And go to the wars with me."
He's drawn her by both hands
  With her face against the sea.

"He that strews red shall gather white,
  He that sows white reap red,
Before your face and my daughter's
  Meet in a marriage-bed.

"Gold coin shall grow in the yellow field,
  Green corn in the green sea-water,
And red fruit grow of the rose's red,
  Ere your fruit grow in her."

"But I shall have her by land," he said,
  "Or I shall have her by sea,
Or I shall have her by strong treason
  And no grace go with me."

Her father's drawn her by both hands,
  He's rent her gown from her,
He's ta'en the smock round her body,
  Cast in the sea-water.

The captain's drawn her by both sides
  Out of the fair green sea;
"Stand up, stand up, thou May Janet,
  And come to the war with me."

The first town they came to
  There was a blue bride-chamber;

He clothed her on with silk
  And belted her with amber.

The second town they came to
  The bridesmen feasted knee to knee;
He clothed her on with silver,
  A stately thing to see.

The third town they came to
  The bridesmaids all had gowns of gold;
He clothed her on with purple,
  A rich thing to behold.

The last town they came to
  He clothed her white and red,
With a green flag either side of her
  And a gold flag overhead.

THE BLOODY SON

(FINNISH)

"O where have ye been the morn sae late,
  My merry son, come tell me hither?
O where have ye been the morn sae late?
  And I wot I hae not anither."
"By the water-gate, by the water-gate,
  O dear mither."

"And whatten kin' o' wark had ye there to make,
  My merry son, come tell me hither?
And whatten kin' o' wark had ye there to make?
  And I wot I hae not anither."
"I watered my steeds with water frae the lake,
  O dear mither."

"Why is your coat sae fouled the day,
  My merry son, come tell me hither?
Why is your coat sae fouled the day?
  And I wot I hae not anither."
"The steeds were stamping sair by the weary banks of clay,
  O dear mither."

"And where gat ye thae sleeves of red,
  My merry son, come tell me hither?
And where gat ye thae sleeves of red?
  And I wot I hae not anither."
"I have slain my ae brither by the weary waterhead,
  O dear mither."

"And where will ye gang to mak your mend,
  My merry son, come tell me hither?
And where will ye gang to mak your mend?

And I wot I hae not anither."
"The warldis way, to the warldis end,
  O dear mither."

"And what will ye leave your father dear,
  My merry son, come tell me hither?
And what will ye leave your father dear?
  And I wot I hae not anither."
"The wood to fell and the logs to bear,
For he'll never see my body mair,
  O dear mither."

"And what will ye leave your mither dear,
  My merry son, come tell me hither?
And what will ye leave your mither dear?
  And I wot I hae not anither."
"The wool to card and the wool to wear,
For ye'll never see my body mair,
  O dear mither."

"And what will ye leave for your wife to take,
  My merry son, come tell me hither?
And what will ye leave for your wife to take?
  And I wot I hae not anither."
"A goodly gown and a fair new make,
For she'll do nae mair for my body's sake,
  O dear mither."

"And what will ye leave your young son fair,
  My merry son, come tell me hither?
And what will ye leave your young son fair?
  And I wot ye hae not anither."
"A twiggen school-rod for his body to bear,
Though it garred him greet he'll get nae mair,
  O dear mither."

"And what will ye leave your little daughter sweet,
  My merry son, come tell me hither?
And what will ye leave your little daughter sweet?
  And I wot ye hae not anither."
"Wild mulberries for her mouth to eat,
She'll get nae mair though it garred her greet,
  O dear mither."

"And when will ye come back frae roamin',
  My merry son, come tell me hither?
And when will ye come back frae roamin'?
  And I wot I hae not anither."
"When the sunrise out of the north is comen,
  O dear mither."

"When shall the sunrise on the north side be,
  My merry son, come tell me hither?
When shall the sunrise on the north side be?
  And I wot I hae not anither."
"When chuckie-stanes shall swim in the sea,
  O dear mither."

"When shall stanes in the sea swim,
  My merry son, come tell me hither?
When shall stanes in the sea swim?
  And I wot I hae not anither."
"When birdies' feathers are as lead therein,
  O dear mither."

"When shall feathers be as lead,
  My merry son, come tell me hither?
When shall feathers be as lead?
  And I wot I hae not anither."
"When God shall judge between the quick and dead,
  O dear mither."

THE SEA-SWALLOWS

This fell when Christmas lights were done,
  (Red rose leaves will never make wine)
But before the Easter lights begun;
  The ways are sair fra' the Till to the Tyne.

Two lovers sat where the rowan blows
  And all the grass is heavy and fine,
By the gathering-place of the sea-swallows
  When the wind brings them over Tyne.

Blossom of broom will never make bread,
  Red rose leaves will never make wine;
Between her brows she is grown red,
  That was full white in the fields by Tyne.

"O what is this thing ye have on,
  Show me now, sweet daughter of mine?"
"O father, this is my little son
  That I found hid in the sides of Tyne.

"O what will ye give my son to eat,
  Red rose leaves will never make wine?"
"Fen-water and adder's meat."
  The ways are sair fra' the Till to the Tyne.

"Or what will ye get my son to wear?"
  (Red rose leaves will never make wine.)
"A weed and a web of nettle's hair."
  The ways are sair fra' the Till to the Tyne.

"Or what will ye take to line his bed?"
  (Red rose leaves will never make wine.)
"Two black stones at the kirkwall's head."

 The ways are sair fra' the Till to the Tyne.

"Or what will ye give my son for land?"
 (Red rose leaves will never make wine.)
"Three girl's paces of red sand."
 The ways are sair fra' the Till to the Tyne.

"Or what will ye give me for my son?"
 (Red rose leaves will never make wine.)
"Six times to kiss his young mouth on."
 The ways are sair fra' the Till to the Tyne.

"But what have ye done with the bearing-bread,
 And what have ye made of the washing-wine?
Or where have ye made your bearing-bed,
 To bear a son in the sides of Tyne?"

"The bearing-bread is soft and new,
 There is no soil in the straining wine;
The bed was made between green and blue,
 It stands full soft by the sides of Tyne.

"The fair grass was my bearing-bread,
 The well-water my washing-wine;
The low leaves were my bearing-bed,
 And that was best in the sides of Tyne."

"O daughter, if ye have done this thing,
 I wot the greater grief is mine;
This was a bitter child-bearing,
 When ye were got by the sides of Tyne.

"About the time of sea-swallows
 That fly full thick by six and nine,
Ye'll have my body out of the house,
 To bury me by the sides of Tyne.

"Set nine stones by the wall for twain,"
  (Red rose leaves will never make wine)
"For the bed I take will measure ten."
  The ways are sair fra' the Till to the Tyne.

"Tread twelve girl's paces out for three,"
  (Red rose leaves will never make wine)
"For the pit I made has taken me."
  The ways are sair fra' the Till to the Tyne.

THE YEAR OF LOVE

There were four loves that one by one,
Following the seasons and the sun,
Passed over without tears, and fell
Away without farewell.

The first was made of gold and tears,
The next of aspen-leaves and fears,
The third of rose-boughs and rose-roots,
The last love of strange fruits.

These were the four loves faded. Hold
Some minutes fast the time of gold
When our lips each way clung and clove
To a face full of love.

The tears inside our eyelids met,
Wrung forth with kissing, and wept wet
The faces cleaving each to each
Where the blood served for speech.

The second, with low patient brows
Bound under aspen-coloured boughs
And eyes made strong and grave with sleep
And yet too weak to weep--

The third, with eager mouth at ease
Fed from late autumn honey, lees
Of scarce gold left in latter cells
With scattered flower-smells--

Hair sprinkled over with spoilt sweet
Of ruined roses, wrists and feet
Slight-swathed, as grassy-girdled sheaves
Hold in stray poppy-leaves--

The fourth, with lips whereon has bled
Some great pale fruit's slow colour, shed
From the rank bitter husk whence drips
Faint blood between her lips--

Made of the heat of whole great Junes
Burning the blue dark round their moons
(Each like a mown red marigold)
So hard the flame keeps hold--

These are burnt thoroughly away.
Only the first holds out a day
Beyond these latter loves that were
Made of mere heat and air.

And now the time is winterly
The first love fades too: none will see,
When April warms the world anew,
The place wherein love grew.

DEDICATION 1865

The sea gives her shells to the shingle,
  The earth gives her streams to the sea:
They are many, but my gift is single,
  My verses, the firstfruits of me.
Let the wind take the green and the grey leaf,
  Cast forth without fruit upon air;
Take rose-leaf and vine-leaf and bay-leaf
  Blown loose from the hair.

The night shakes them round me in legions,
  Dawn drives them before her like dreams;
Time sheds them like snows on strange regions,
  Swept shoreward on infinite streams;
Leaves pallid and sombre and ruddy,
  Dead fruits of the fugitive years;
Some stained as with wine and made bloody,
  And some as with tears.

Some scattered in seven years' traces,
  As they fell from the boy that was then;
Long left among idle green places,
  Or gathered but now among men;
On seas full of wonder and peril,
  Blown white round the capes of the north;
Or in islands where myrtles are sterile
  And loves bring not forth.

O daughters of dreams and of stories
  That life is not wearied of yet,
Faustine, Fragoletta, Dolores,
  Félise and Yolande and Juliette,
Shall I find you not still, shall I miss you,
  When sleep, that is true or that seems,
Comes back to me hopeless to kiss you,

O daughters of dreams?

They are past as a slumber that passes,
  As the dew of a dawn of old time;
More frail than the shadows on glasses,
  More fleet than a wave or a rhyme.
As the waves after ebb drawing seaward,
  When their hollows are full of the night,
So the birds that flew singing to me-ward
  Recede out of sight.

The songs of dead seasons, that wander
  On wings of articulate words;
Lost leaves that the shore-wind may squander,
  Light flocks of untameable birds;
Some sang to me dreaming in class-time
  And truant in hand as in tongue;
For the youngest were born of boy's pastime,
  The eldest are young.

Is there shelter while life in them lingers,
  Is there hearing for songs that recede,
Tunes touched from a harp with man's fingers
  Or blown with boy's mouth in a reed?
Is there place in the land of your labour,
  Is there room in your world of delight,
Where change has not sorrow for neighbour
  And day has not night?

In their wings though the sea-wind yet quivers,
  Will you spare not a space for them there
Made green with the running of rivers
  And gracious with temperate air;
In the fields and the turreted cities,
  That cover from sunshine and rain
Fair passions and bountiful pities

And loves without stain?

In a land of clear colours and stories,
  In a region of shadowless hours,
Where earth has a garment of glories
  And a murmur of musical flowers;
In woods where the spring half uncovers
  The flush of her amorous face,
By the waters that listen for lovers,
  For these is there place?

For the song-birds of sorrow, that muffle
  Their music as clouds do their fire:
For the storm-birds of passion, that ruffle
  Wild wings in a wind of desire;
In the stream of the storm as it settles
  Blown seaward, borne far from the sun,
Shaken loose on the darkness like petals
  Dropt one after one?

Though the world of your hands be more gracious
  And lovelier in lordship of things
Clothed round by sweet art with the spacious
  Warm heaven of her imminent wings,
Let them enter, unfledged and nigh fainting,
  For the love of old loves and lost times;
And receive in your palace of painting
  This revel of rhymes.

Though the seasons of man full of losses
  Make empty the years full of youth,
If but one thing be constant in crosses,
  Change lays not her hand upon truth;
Hopes die, and their tombs are for token
  That the grief as the joy of them ends
Ere time that breaks all men has broken

The faith between friends.

Though the many lights dwindle to one light,
  There is help if the heaven has one;
Though the skies be discrowned of the sunlight
  And the earth dispossessed of the sun,
They have moonlight and sleep for repayment,
  When, refreshed as a bride and set free,
With stars and sea-winds in her raiment,
  Night sinks on the sea.

Fin.

Printed in Great Britain
by Amazon